T0265656

CLEAR
THINKING

CLEAR
THINKING

Turning Ordinary Moments
into Extraordinary Results

SHANE PARRISH

PORTFOLIO | PENGUIN

PORTFOLIO / PENGUIN
An imprint of Penguin Random House LLC
penguinrandomhouse.com

Most Portfolio books are available at a discount when purchased in quantity for sales promotions or corporate use. Special editions, which include personalized covers, excerpts, and corporate imprints, can be created when purchased in large quantities. For more information, please call (212) 572-2232 or e-mail specialmarkets@penguinrandomhouse.com. Your local bookstore can also assist with discounted bulk purchases using the Penguin Random House corporate Business-to-Business program. For assistance in locating a participating retailer, e-mail B2B@penguinrandomhouse.com.

Library of Congress Cataloging-in-Publication Data
Names: Parrish, Shane, author.
Title: Clear thinking : turning ordinary moments into extraordinary results / Shane Parrish.
Description: [New York, NY] : Portfolio/Penguin, [2023] | Includes bibliographical references and index. |
Identifiers: LCCN 2023010817 (print) | LCCN 2023010818 (ebook) | ISBN 9780593086117 (hardcover) | ISBN 9780593716212 (international edition) | ISBN 9780593086124 (ebook)
Subjects: LCSH: Decision making.
Classification: LCC BF448 .P38 2023 (print) | LCC BF448 (ebook) | DDC 153.8/3--dc23/eng/20230616
LC record available at https://lccn.loc.gov/2023010817
LC ebook record available at https://lccn.loc.gov/2023010818

Printed in the United States of America
7   9   10   8   6

BOOK DESIGN BY TANYA MAIBORODA

Contents

Preface

I STARTED WORKING AT AN INTELLIGENCE AGENCY IN AU-gust 2001. A few weeks later, the world changed forever.

Everyone at the agency suddenly found themselves thrust into positions and responsibilities they weren't ready for. My job involved constantly figuring out how to do things few had even imagined possible. Not only did I need to solve complicated and new problems, but people's lives were at stake. Failure was not an option.

One night, I was walking home at 3:00 a.m. after one of our operations. The outcome wasn't what I had hoped for. I knew I'd have to face my boss in the morning and explain what happened and what I'd been thinking when I made the choices I did.

Had I thought everything through clearly? Was there something I missed? How was I to know?

My thinking would be laid bare for everyone to see and judge.

I walked into my boss's office the next day and explained what went through my mind. When I finished, I told him I wasn't ready for this job or the level of responsibility it required. He put his pen down, drew a deep breath, and said, "No one is ready for this job, Shane. But you and this team are all we got."

His response wasn't exactly comforting. By "team" he meant twelve people working eighty hours a week for years. By "all we got" he meant starting the most important new program the agency had seen in generations. I walked away from our brief encounter with my head spinning.

That night I started asking myself questions that I'd continue exploring for the next decade. How can we get better at reasoning? Why do people make bad decisions? Why do some people consistently get better results than others who have the same information? How can I be right more often, and decrease the probability of a bad outcome when lives are on the line?

Up until that point in my career, I'd been fairly lucky, and while I wanted that luck to continue, I also wanted to depend on it less. If there was a method for clear thinking and good judgment—I wanted to harness it.

If you're like me, no one ever taught you how to think or make decisions. There's no class called Clear Thinking 101 in school. Everyone seems to expect you to know how to do it already or to learn how on your own. As it turns out, though, learning about thinking—thinking *clearly*—is surprisingly hard.

For the next several years, I devoted myself to learning how to think better. I watched how people acquired information, reasoned, and acted in practice, and how their actions unfolded into positive or negative outcomes. Were some people just smarter than others? Or did they have better systems or practices in place? In the moments that mattered, were people even aware of the quality of their thinking? How could I avoid the obvious errors?

I followed the most senior people around to meetings. I'd sit there quietly* listening to what they thought was important and why. I read anything I could on cognition and talked to anyone who would pick up the phone.

I sought out the titans of industry† who seemed to consistently think clearly even when others couldn't. They seemed to know something that was not commonly known, and I was determined to find out what.

While the rest of us are chasing victory, the best in the world know they must avoid losing before they can win. It turns out this is a surprisingly effective strategy.

To catalog my learning, I created an anonymous website called Farnam Street, found at fs.blog, named in honor of Charlie Munger and Warren Buffett,‡ two people who exercise judgment for a living and who have had a profound impact on how I see the world.§

I've been fortunate over the years to talk to my heroes Charlie Munger and Daniel Kahneman about thinking and

---

* Okay, mostly quietly.

† Working for an intelligence agency opens a lot of doors that you might think are closed.

‡ The headquarters for Berkshire Hathaway, where Warren Buffett is CEO and Charlie Munger is vice chairman, is on Farnam Street in Omaha, Nebraska, USA.

§ I made it anonymous because, it turns out, three-letter agencies tend to frown on public profiles. Things have changed since those days. With all the trouble they have recruiting, you can have a public profile now. In fact, while job descriptions are vague, people often put the name of the agency they work for in their LinkedIn profile now. It's important to realize when I started, we didn't exist—there was no sign on the building. The idea of having any public profile was over a decade away.

decision-making, along with other master practitioners like Bill Ackman, Annie Duke, Adam Robinson, Randall Stutman, and Kat Cole. Many of these conversations are public on *The Knowledge Project* podcast. Others, like my time spent with Munger, must remain private. Among all the people I've spoken with, though, no one has influenced my thinking and ideas more than my friend Peter D. Kaufman.

Thousands of conversations have yielded a key insight.

In order to get the results we desire, we must do two things. We must first create the space to reason in our thoughts, feelings, and actions; and second, we must deliberately use that space to think clearly. Once you have mastered this skill, you will find you have an unstoppable advantage.

Decisions made through clear thinking will put you in increasingly better positions, and success will only compound from there.

This book is a practical guide to mastering clear thinking.

The first half of the book is about creating space for it. First, we identify the enemies of clear thinking. You will learn how most of what we consider to be "thinking" is in fact reacting without reasoning, prompted by biological instincts that evolved to preserve our species. When we react without reasoning, our position is weakened, and our options get increasingly worse. When we ritualize a response to our biological triggers, we create the space to think clearly, and strengthen our position. Then, we identify a number of practical, actionable ways to both manage your weaknesses and build your strengths so that space is consistently created when you're under pressure.

The second half of the book is about putting clear thinking into practice. Once you are in a place where you've shored up your strengths and managed your weaknesses—when you've created the pause between thought and action—you can turn clear thinking into effective decisions. In Part 4 I share the most practical tools you can use to solve problems.

Finally, once you have mastered the skills of making your defaults work for instead of against you and maximizing the tool that is your rational mind, I'll turn to perhaps the most important question of all: the question of what your goals are in the first place. All the successful execution in the world is worthless if it's not in service of the right outcome, but how do you decide what that is?

Along the way, I'll show you the most effective approaches to thinking in a way few people talk about. We won't use fancy jargon, spreadsheets, or decision trees. Instead, we'll focus on the practical skills I've learned from others, discovered on my own, and tested on thousands of people from various organizations, cultures, and industries.

Together we'll uncover the missing link between behavioral science and real-world results and turn ordinary moments into extraordinary results.

The lessons in this book are simple, practical, and timeless. They draw heavily on the wisdom of others and my own lived experience putting them into practice. I relied on these lessons and insights to make better decisions inside the intelligence agency, build and scale multiple businesses, and surprisingly become a better parent. How you use them is up to you.

If there is a tagline to my life, it is "Mastering the best of what other people have already figured out," and this book is a tribute to that belief. I've done my best to attribute those ideas to the people who deserve the credit. I've probably missed some, and for that I apologize. When you put things into practice, they become part of you. After two decades, thousands of conversations with the best in the world, and more books devoured than I can count, it's not easy to remember where everything comes from. Most of it has just been ingrained into my unconscious. It's safe to assume that anything useful in this book is someone else's idea, and that my main contribution is to put the mosaic of what I've learned from others who came before me out there for the world.

The Power of Clear Thinking
in Ordinary Moments

WHAT HAPPENS IN ORDINARY MOMENTS DETERMINES your future.

We're taught to focus on the big decisions, rather than the moments where we don't even realize we're making a choice. Yet these ordinary moments often matter more to our success than the big decisions. This can be difficult to appreciate.

We think that if only we get the big things right, everything will magically fall into place. If we choose to marry the right person, it'll all be okay. If we choose the right career, we'll be happy. If we pick the right investment, we'll be rich. This wisdom is, at best, partially true. You can marry the most amazing person in the world, but if you take them for granted, it will end. You can pick the best career, but if you don't work your butt off, you won't get opportunities. You can find the perfect investment, only to look at your savings account and have nothing to invest. Even when we get the big decisions directionally right, we're not guaranteed to get the results we want.

We don't think of ordinary moments as decisions. No one taps us on the shoulder as we react to a comment by a coworker to tell us that we're about to pour either gasoline or water onto this flame. Of course, if we knew we were about to make the situation worse, we wouldn't. No one tries to win the moment at the expense of the decade, and yet that is often how it goes.

The enemies of clear thinking—the more primal parts of our nature—make it hard to see what's happening and instead just make our lives more challenging. When we react with emotion to a colleague in a meeting, we must make amends. When we make a decision to prove we're right rather than get the best outcome possible, we only end up with a mess to clean up later. If we start bickering with our partner on Friday, the entire weekend can be lost. No wonder we have less energy, more stress, and feel busy all the time.

In most ordinary moments the situation thinks for us. We don't realize it at the time because these moments seem so insignificant. However, as days turn into weeks and weeks into months, the accumulation of these moments makes accomplishing our goals easier or harder.

Each moment puts you in a better or worse position to handle the future. It's that positioning that eventually makes life easier or harder. When our ego takes over and we show someone we're the boss, we make the future harder. When we are passive-aggressive with a colleague at work, our relationship becomes worse. And while these moments don't seem to matter much at the time, they compound into our current position. And our position determines our future.

A good position allows you to think clearly rather than be forced by circumstances into a decision. One reason the best in the world make consistently good decisions is they rarely find themselves forced into a decision by circumstances.

You don't need to be smarter than others to outperform them if you can out-position them. Anyone looks like a genius when they're in a good position, and even the smartest person looks like an idiot when they're in a bad one.

The greatest aid to judgment is starting from a good position. The company with cash on the balance sheet and low debt has nothing but good options to choose from. When bad times come, and they always do, their options go from good to great. On the other hand, a company with no cash and high debt has nothing but bad options to choose from. Things quickly go from bad to worse. And this example easily extends beyond the boardroom as well.

Time is the friend of someone who is properly positioned and the enemy of someone poorly positioned. When you are well positioned, there are many paths to victory. If you are poorly positioned, there may be only one. You can think of this a bit like playing *Tetris*. When you play well, you have many options for where to put the next piece. When you play poorly, you need just the right piece.

What a lot of people miss is that ordinary moments determine your position, and your position determines your options. Clear thinking is the key to proper positioning, which is what allows you to master your circumstances rather than be mastered by them.

It doesn't matter what position you find yourself in right now. What matters is whether you improve your position today.

Every ordinary moment is an opportunity to make the future easier or harder. It all depends on whether you're thinking clearly.

PART 1

THE ENEMIES OF CLEAR THINKING

Never forget that your unconscious is smarter than you, faster than you, and more powerful than you. It may even control you. You will never know all of its secrets.

—CORDELIA FINE,
A Mind of Its Own: How Your Brain Distorts and Deceives

THE FIRST THING I heard was shouting. Generally, this is not what you expect to hear when approaching the CEO's office. This CEO was different.

I walked into his office, put my briefcase on the table, and sat down directly across from him. He didn't acknowledge my presence. While months of working for him had led me to expect as much, it was still unsettling.

I was his designated right hand, and almost nothing and no one got to him without going through me first. That's what made this call so interesting. It wasn't on his calendar.

Whomever he was talking with, the conversation had turned him red with rage. I had already learned the hard way not to interrupt him during moments like this with a nudge to take a breath. If I did, his wrath would quickly direct itself at me.

As he hung up, his eyes met mine. I knew I had a split second to say something, or he'd start yelling at me for having to take this unscheduled call.

"What was that all about?" I asked.

"They needed to be put in their place," he said.

I didn't know who had been on the other end of the phone, but the pitch of his anger led me to believe it was someone unfamiliar with him. The people who worked for this CEO knew it was easier not to tell him anything that might upset him. This included bad news, ideas that clashed with his beliefs, and of course a nudge to stop when he was making a situation worse.

It would be one of the last calls he ever took in his office. This ordinary moment changed everything.

It turned out, the person on the other end of that phone call was desperately trying to report a problem with serious consequences for the organization. When their concern was met with wrath that day, they decided to take their concerns to the board. Not long afterward, the CEO was fired.

While part of me wants to tell you it was directly because of his behavior, we both know that wouldn't be true. He was fired for not acting on the very information the person on the other end of the phone was trying to tell him, because his ego wouldn't allow for it. If he had been thinking clearly, he might still have his job.*

●

* Some details of this story have been changed to protect the identity of the person involved. The general trajectory remains true.

Thinking Badly— or Not Thinking at All?

RATIONALITY IS WASTED IF YOU DON'T KNOW *WHEN* TO use it.

When you ask people about improving thinking, they typically point toward numerous tools designed to help people think more rationally. Bookstores are full of books that assume the problem is our ability to reason. They list the steps we should take and the tools we should use to exercise better judgment. If you know you should be thinking, these can be helpful.

What I've learned from watching real people in action is that, just like the angry CEO, they're often unaware circumstances are thinking for them. It's as if we expect the inner voice in our head to say, "STOP! THIS IS A MOMENT WHEN YOU NEED TO THINK!"

And because we don't know we should be thinking, we cede control to our impulses.

In the space between stimulus and response, one of two things can happen. You can consciously pause and apply reason to the situation. Or you can cede control and execute a default behavior.

The problem is, our default behavior often makes things worse.

When someone slights us, we lash out with angry words.

When someone cuts us off, we assume malice on their part.

When things go slower than we want, we become frustrated and impatient.

When someone is passive-aggressive, we take the bait and escalate.

In these moments of reaction, we don't realize that our brains have been hijacked by our biology, and that the outcome will go against what we seek. We don't realize that hoarding information to gain an advantage is hurting the team. We don't realize we're conforming to the group's ideas when we should be thinking for ourselves. We don't realize our emotions are making us react in ways that create problems downstream.

So our first step in improving our outcomes is to train ourselves to identify the moments when judgment is called for in the first place, and pause to create space to think clearly. This training takes a lot of time and effort, because it involves counterbalancing our hardwired biological defaults evolved over many centuries. But mastery over the ordinary moments that make the future easier or harder is not only possible, it's the critical ingredient to success and achieving your long-term goals.

The High Cost of Losing Control

Reacting without reasoning makes every situation worse.

Consider a common scenario that I've seen countless times. A coworker slights a project you're leading in a meeting. Instinctively you hit back with a comment that undermines them or their work. You didn't make a conscious choice to respond, you just did. Before you even know what's happening, the damage is done. Not only does the relationship suffer but the meeting goes sideways.

Too much energy is then consumed getting you back to where you were. The relationship needs to be repaired. The derailed meeting needs to be rescheduled. You might need to talk to the other people in the meeting to clear the air. And even after all of this, you might still be worse off than you were before. Every witness and every person they talked to about what happened received an unconscious signal that eroded their trust in you. Rebuilding that trust takes months of consistent behavior.

All the time and energy you spend fixing your unforced errors comes at the expense of moving toward the outcomes you want. There is a huge advantage in having more of your energy instead go toward achieving your goals instead of fixing your problems. The person who learns how to think clearly ultimately applies more of their overall effort toward the outcomes they want than the person who doesn't.

You have little hope of thinking clearly, though, if you can't manage your defaults.

Biological Instincts

There's nothing stronger than biological instincts. They control us often without us even knowing. Failing to come to terms with them only makes you more susceptible to their influence.

If you're having trouble understanding why you sometimes react to situations in the worst possible way, the problem isn't your mind. Your mind is doing exactly what biology programmed it to do: act quickly and efficiently in response to threats, without wasting valuable time thinking.

If someone breaks into your house, you instinctively stand between them and your kids. If someone approaches you with a menacing expression, you tense up. If you sense your job is at risk, you might unconsciously start hoarding information. Your animal brain believes you can't be fired if you're the only one who knows how to do your job. Biology, not your rational mind, told you what to do.

When our unthinking reactions make situations worse, that little voice in our head starts to beat us up: "What were you thinking, you idiot?" The truth of the matter is, you weren't thinking. You were reacting, exactly like the animal you are. Your mind wasn't in charge. Your biology was.

Our biological tendencies are hardwired within us.* Those tendencies often served our prehistoric ancestors well, but they tend to get in our way today. These timeless behaviors have been described and discussed by philosophers and scientists from Aristotle and the Stoics to Daniel Kahneman and Jonathan Haidt.[1]

For instance, like all animals, **we are naturally prone to defend our territory**.[2] We might not be defending a piece of terrain on the African savanna, but territory isn't just physical, it's also psychological. Our identity is part of our territory too. When someone criticizes our work, status, or how we see ourselves, we instinctively shut down or defend ourselves. When someone challenges our beliefs, we stop listening and go on the attack. No thoughts, just pure animal instinct.

---

* Thank you, Peter Kaufman, for the many conversations we've had on this that informed my thinking.

We're naturally wired to organize the world into a hierarchy. We do this to help make sense of the world, maintain our beliefs, and generally feel better. But when someone infringes on our place in the world and our understanding of how it works, we react without thinking. When someone cuts you off on the highway and road rage kicks in, that's your unconscious mind saying, "Who are you to cut me off?" You're reacting to a threat to your inherent sense of hierarchy. On the road we are all equals. We're all supposed to play by the same rules. Cutting someone off violates those rules and implies higher status.* Or consider when you get frustrated with your kids and end an argument with "Because I said so." (Or the office equivalent: "Because I'm the boss.") In these moments you've stopped thinking and regressed to your biological tendencies of reaffirming the hierarchy.

We're self-preserving. Most of us would never intentionally push someone else down to get where we want to go.† The key word here is "intentionally," because intention involves thought. When we're triggered and not thinking, our desire to protect ourselves first takes over. When layoffs loom at a company, otherwise decent people will quickly throw each other under the bus to keep a job. Sure, they wouldn't consciously want to hurt their colleagues, but if it comes down to "them versus me," they will ensure they come out on top. That's biology.

Our biological instincts provide an automatic response without conscious processing. After all, that's what they're for!

Conscious processing takes both time and energy. Evolution favored stimulus-response shortcuts because they're ad-

---

* I am pretty sure I first heard this example from Jim Rohn but can't find the specific reference.
† Except, of course, whomever the song "Better Than Revenge" by Taylor Swift was written for.

vantageous for the group: they enhance *group* fitness, *group* survival, and reproduction. As humans continued flourishing in groups, hierarchies developed, creating order out of chaos and giving us all a place. Territory is how we tried to avoid fighting others—you stay out of my territory, I'll stay out of yours. And self-preservation means we choose survival over rules, norms, or customs.

The problem occurs when you zoom in from the aggregate to the individual, from the eons of evolution to the present moment of decision. In today's world, basic survival is no longer in question. The very tendencies that once served us now often act as an anchor holding us in place, weakening our position, and making things harder than they need to be.

Knowing Your Defaults

While there are many such instincts, four stand out to me as the most prominent, the most distinctive, and the most dangerous. These behaviors represent something akin to our brain's default or factory settings.[3] They're behavioral programs written into our DNA by natural selection that our brains will automatically execute when triggered unless we stop and take the time to think. They have many names, but for the purposes of this book, let's call them *the emotion default*, *the ego default*, *the social default*, and *the inertia default*.

Here's how each essentially functions:

1. The emotion default: we tend to respond to feelings rather than reasons and facts.
2. The ego default: we tend to react to anything that threatens our sense of self-worth or our position in a group hierarchy.

3. The social default: we tend to conform to the norms of our larger social group.

4. The inertia default: we're habit forming and comfort seeking. We tend to resist change, and to prefer ideas, processes, and environments that are familiar.

There are no hard edges between defaults; they often bleed into one another. Each on their own is enough to cause unforced errors, but when they act together, things quickly go from bad to worse.

People who master their defaults get the best real-world results. It's not that they don't have a temper or an ego, they just know how to control both rather than be controlled by them. With the ability to think clearly in ordinary moments today, they consistently put themselves in a good position for tomorrow.

In the following section I'll give an overview of how these defaults manifest in human behavior, and how to recognize when they're at play in your own life. Not only will your own past actions make more sense after taking defaults into account, but you'll also learn to identify when others are reacting to them too.

The Emotion Default

THE GODFATHER IS ONE OF MY FAVORITE MOVIES, IN PART because of the many business lessons it contains. Vito Corleone, head of the Corleone crime family, is a master of patience and discipline. With his defaults under control, he never reacts without reasoning, and when he does react, it's ruthlessly effective.

Vito's oldest son, Santino, a.k.a. Sonny, is Vito's heir apparent. Unlike his father, however, Sonny is vengeful, impulsive, and hotheaded. He easily flies into fits of rage, reacting first and reasoning later. His unforced errors ensure he's constantly playing life on hard mode.

The emotion default controls Sonny, and he doesn't realize it. On one occasion, he beats his brother-in-law, Carlo Rizzi, in public, an act that will have unintended future consequences. On another occasion, a rival family approaches Vito about partnering to sell drugs. Vito declines. But Sonny, quick to react without thinking, jumps in and undermines his father's position. After the meeting, Vito offers his son a lesson: "Never tell anyone outside the family what you're thinking again."

But the lesson comes too late; the damage is already done. The dealer decides that if Vito can be taken out, Sonny will take the deal. Sonny's indiscretion leads to an assassination attempt on Vito's life, which critically wounds his father.

While Vito is in the hospital, Sonny becomes acting head of the family. True to his impulsive nature, he initiates an all-out war with the other families. Meanwhile, Carlo Rizzi continues to resent Sonny for beating him in front of his crew, and conspires with a rival family to kill him. Carlo baits Sonny into reacting without reasoning, which leads to Sonny's brutal assassination on the Jones Beach Causeway.

Sonny's quick temper ultimately leads to his downfall, as it does for many people. When we respond without reasoning, we're more likely to make mistakes that seem obvious in hindsight. In fact, when we respond emotionally, we often don't even realize that we're in a position that calls for thinking at all. When you are possessed by the moment, all the reasoning tools in the world won't help you.

From Emotion to Action

There's a bit of Sonny in each of us. You experience anger, fear, or some other emotion, and feel compelled to act immediately. But in these moments, the action you're pushed toward rarely serves you.

Anger at a rival prevents you from doing what's in your own best interest. Fear of losing an opportunity pushes you to cut thinking short and act impulsively. Outrage at a criticism causes you to lash out in defense, alienating potential allies. The list goes on.

Emotions can multiply all of your progress by zero. It doesn't matter how much you've thought about or worked at something, it can all be undone in an instant. No one is immune. The Olympian Matthew Emmons, for instance, was a prodigy who'd come to dominate the field of competitive rifle shooting. He was poised to win his second Olympic gold when the emotion default worked its mischief. Emmons was in the final round. He aimed. He fired. Bullseye. The only problem: he shot at the wrong target! Had it been the right one, he would've won the gold. Instead, he was awarded zero points and slipped to eighth place.

Afterward, Emmons said that he usually looked through the rifle scope at the number above the target to make sure it was the correct one before lowering the rifle to the bullseye. In this case, he'd skipped that crucial first step.

"On that shot," he said, "I was just worrying about calming myself down . . . so I didn't even look at the number."[1] So he scored a point for the emotion default, instead.

While Emmons's Olympic loss is epic, it pales in comparison to the tragedy that unfolded in the life of a former colleague of mine. Let's call him Steve. I noticed that Steve always seemed to shut down whenever politics came up during work dinners. One day, away from the group, I asked him why.

He told me a story I'd never forget.

One night, Steve's parents came over for dinner. When they started talking about politics and taxes, the conversation grew heated. Steve's emotions soon took over, and he started saying things he probably didn't mean. Things that couldn't be unsaid. Things we might say when we're reacting and not thinking.

That was the last conversation he ever had with his parents. On their way home, their car was struck head on by a drunk driver. Neither recovered. That night still haunts Steve to this day. It's a memory that won't go away, about an ordinary moment he'll forever regret.

Emotions can make even the best of us into idiots, driving us away from clear thinking. They often have help, though. Later we'll see some of the many inbuilt biological vulnerabilities that leave us even more exposed to the emotion default's influence: sleep deprivation, hunger, fatigue, emotion, distraction, stress from feeling rushed, and being in an unfamiliar environment. If you find yourself in any of these conditions, be on your guard! The emotion default is likely running the show. We'll also explore the safeguards that can protect you in such situations.

CHAPTER 1.3

The Ego Default

GOING BACK TO *THE GODFATHER,* CARLO RIZZI IS AN EX-
ample of a different default at work: the ego.

Carlo becomes a member of the Corleone family when he
marries Vito's daughter, Connie. As an outsider, he occupies a
relatively low position in the social hierarchy. Full of pride and
ego, he becomes increasingly frustrated by his marginal role in
the family business. This frustration leads him to take some
unforgivable actions.

That's just what happens in life sometimes; the ego default prompts us to promote and protect our self-image at all
costs.

In Carlo's case, being reminded of his low status in the
family combines with his desire to defend his self-image (*"I can
do more than the job I'm in, but they won't give me more"*) and
leads him to make the ultimate betrayal. Carlo never intended
to tear the Corleone family apart from within. He just wanted
a role in line with how he saw himself. The daily indignation
of being treated as lesser set off a chain reaction he never intended.

Appearing Successful vs. Being Successful

Not all confidence is created equally. Sometimes, it comes from a track record of applying deep knowledge successfully, and other times it comes from the shallowness of reading an article. It's amazing how often the ego turns unearned knowledge into reckless confidence.

A little knowledge can be a dangerous thing, as one of my kids learned the hard way. Not wanting to write out his homework in French, which would take a lot of time and effort, he realized he could write it out in English and put it through an online translator. When I asked him how he finished so quickly, he told me it was easy and left it at that. Of course, his French teacher realized what he had done and gave him a zero.

Our ego tempts us into thinking we're more than we are. Left unchecked, it can turn confidence into overconfidence or even arrogance. We get a bit of knowledge on the internet and suddenly we are full of hubris. Everything seems easy. As a result, we take risks that we may not understand we're taking. We must resist this kind of unearned confidence, though, if we are to get the results we desire.

Recently, after a talk I attended on the growing homeless population, the person sitting next to me commented on how easy it would be to solve this deep and complex issue. He was intoxicated with a little unearned confidence, based on shallow understanding, so the problem seemed simple to him. However, those with competence based on hard-earned knowledge didn't think the problem was simple at all. They were fully aware of the realities of the situation.

Unearned knowledge rushes us to judgment. "I've got this," we think. We convince ourselves that low-chance events are zero-chance events and think only of best-case outcomes. We feel immune to bad luck—to the bad things that happen to other people, because of our newfound (and false) sense of confidence.[1]

Confidence doesn't make bad outcomes any less likely or good outcomes more likely, it only blinds us to risk. The ego also makes us more concerned with maintaining or improving our perceived position in a social hierarchy than with extending our knowledge or skills.

One reason people find it hard to empower others at work is that having them depend on us for every decision makes us feel important and indispensable. Having them depend on us makes us feel not only necessary but powerful. The more people who depend on us the more powerful we feel. However, this position is often self-defeating. Slowly and then all at once we become a prisoner of the circumstances we created; more and more effort is needed to stay in the same place, and we approach the ceiling of brute force.* It's only a matter of time until things break.

The person who wants to be seen as great shows the world how to manipulate them. We're prone to being less concerned with actual greatness than with exuding the appearance of greatness. When someone steps on how we see ourselves (or how we *want* to be seen), the ego leaps into action, and we often react without reasoning. Carlo Rizzi is a fictional example, but there are many real ones.

In September 1780, for instance, the American general Benedict Arnold secretly met a British spy. In exchange for £20,000 and a British military command, Arnold agreed to give the British control of the fort at West Point, which was then under his command.

---

* A phrase I learned from Brent Beshore.

What powerful force could make someone betray his country? Arnold's reason was the same as Carlo Rizzi's: long-harbored resentment about his social standing.

Arnold had been an accomplished military officer, but he wasn't generally well-liked. He had a jealous disposition and frequently complained about Congress promoting younger, less competent officers ahead of him. He was quick to react to social slights, both real and imagined. And his tendency to prove his superiority by humiliating people with whom he disagreed created an invisible army of enemies.

He nevertheless managed to earn the confidence of the Continental Army's commander in chief, George Washington, who appointed Arnold military governor of Philadelphia. Around this time, Arnold sought the hand of Peggy Shippen, the daughter of a wealthy Philadelphia family.

The Shippens were loyalist sympathizers interested in making connections only with similarly wealthy people. Arnold, however, was not wealthy. His alcoholic father had squandered the family fortune when Arnold was a boy. Arnold had been trying to reestablish the family's position in society ever since.

Arnold lived extravagantly, throwing lavish parties, with the hope of earning the respect of Philadelphia's wealthy elite. He promised the Shippens that he would bestow on Peggy a large sum in advance of their wedding as proof of his financial means, and took out a large mortgage to purchase a mansion. When Arnold and Peggy were finally married, Arnold was deeply in debt. He and Peggy couldn't even occupy that mansion because he needed to rent it out to pay the mortgage.

Arnold's lifestyle caught the attention of his many enemies, including Pennsylvania's unscrupulous president of the Supreme Executive Council, Joseph Reed. Reed built a flimsy case against Arnold which, it seemed, was more intended to disgrace the man publicly than anything else. It turned out, however, that Arnold had been using his position as military governor to benefit himself financially. Eventually, his case was brought before a court martial. General Washington gave Arnold only a light reprimand, yet Arnold felt that Washington had betrayed him.

A short while later, he would go on to betray his country.

Arnold's pride had been wounded. He wanted to show others his value and importance. He wanted others to see him the way he saw himself. When they didn't, he stopped exercising judgment, and ended up going down in history for all the wrong reasons.

Who hasn't found themselves in a similar situation? Someone close to you doesn't appreciate you the way you want to be appreciated. Perhaps they don't see how insightful you are. Or maybe they don't see how much you do for them. Desperate to satisfy the ego, either personally or professionally, you stop thinking and do things you otherwise wouldn't, like approach a competitor or flirt with someone at a party. One example I've seen too many times in the workplace is when you stop putting in 100 percent of what you are capable of because you feel underappreciated.* The ego grabs your unconscious, throws your long-term goals out the window, and sets you sailing on a path toward destruction.

If Arnold hadn't been so consumed by ego—had he instead reacted less and reasoned more—he might have seen that his long-term political objectives and his family's well-being demanded a more modest way of life.

---

* While this behavior has been around for a while, during the COVID pandemic of 2020, people started calling this quiet quitting.

Feeling Right over Being Right

Our desire to feel right overpowers our desire to be right.

The ego default urges us to feel right at the expense of being right. Few things feel better than being right—so much so that we will unconsciously rearrange the world into arbitrary hierarchies to maintain our beliefs and feel better about ourselves. My first memory of doing so dates back to my days of working in a grocery store at age sixteen.

One particular customer would always treat the staff poorly. He'd drive up in his fancy car, park it illegally outside, and run in to get something. When there was a line, he'd rudely comment and raise his voice telling everyone to hurry up. We called him Mr. Rolex.

One day when he was waiting in my line, he told me to "hurry the f**k up because this Rolex doesn't pay for itself."

I'll leave my reply out but let's just say that it cost me a job.

It was worth it, though, because the experience made me realize that some people organize their unconscious hierarchy by money and status. Those were the ways Mr. Rolex had of keeping the score to always come out on top.

I remember walking home that night thinking that while I might not have a job, at least I wasn't like him. And at that moment I rearranged the world in such a way that I, the newly unemployed high school student without a car or a lavish wristwatch, came out on top. I had unconsciously organized the world in a way where I could be above him and feel better about myself.

Both of us reverted to the ego default that day.

Most people go through life assuming that they're right . . . and that people who don't see things their way are wrong.[2] We mistake how we want the world to be with how it actually is.

The subject doesn't matter: we're right about politics, other people, our memories; you name it. We mistake how we want the world to work for how it does work.

Of course, we can't be right about everything all the time. Everyone makes mistakes or misremembers some things. But we still want to *feel* right all the time, and ideally get other people to reinforce that feeling. Hence, we channel inordinate amounts of energy to proving to others—or ourselves—that we're right. When this happens, we're less concerned with outcomes and more concerned with protecting our egos.

Later I'll discuss more about how to combat the ego default. For the time being, keep in mind how to recognize it when it rears its head. If you find yourself expending tremendous energy on how you are seen, if you often feel your pride being wounded, if you find yourself reading an article or two on a subject and thinking you're an expert, if you always try to prove you're right and have difficulty admitting mistakes, if you have a hard time saying "I don't know," or if you're frequently envious of others or feel as though you're never given the recognition you deserve—be on guard! Your ego is in charge.

The Social Default

Where all think alike, no one thinks very much.

—WALTER LIPPMANN,
The Stakes of Diplomacy

YEARS AGO, I WITNESSED A PARTICULARLY UGLY AND grim talk at a conference. When it ended, others started clapping. I hesitated but tentatively joined them anyway. It would have felt awkward not to.*

The social default inspires conformity. It coaxes us to fall in line with an idea or behavior simply because other people do. It embodies what the term "social pressure" refers to: wanting

---

* Perhaps not surprisingly, the simple act of clapping has been used and abused by leaders throughout history. Professional clappers, called a claque, would often be positioned in theaters or opera houses. Claques have been used since at least emperor Nero, whose performances were often applauded by thousands of soldiers. Once a few people start clapping, our social default takes hold and we find ourselves, much like I did, clapping without knowing why.

to belong to the crowd, fear of being an outsider, fear of being scorned, fear of disappointing other people.

Our desire to fit in with the group comes from our history. Group interests were well served from a high level of conformity. But so too were our individual interests. Survival inside the tribe was hard but survival outside the tribe was impossible. Because we needed the group, our individual interests became secondary to the group interests. Though the world we live in today is very different from the one we evolved from, we still look to others for cues on how to behave.

The social rewards for going with the crowd are felt long before the benefits of going against it are gained. One measure of a person is the degree to which they'll do the right thing when it goes against the popular belief. However, it is easy to overestimate our willingness to diverge from the crowd, and underestimate our biological instinct to fit in.

The social default encourages us to outsource our thoughts, beliefs, and outcomes to others. When everyone else is doing something, it's easy to rationalize doing it too. No need to stand out, take responsibility for outcomes, or think for yourself. Just put your brain on autopilot and take a nap.

The social default inspires virtue signaling—getting other people to accept or praise your professed beliefs. Especially when there is no cost to such signals.

Princeton professor Robert George wrote, "I sometimes ask students what their position on slavery would have been had they been white and living in the South before abolition. Guess what? They all would have been abolitionists! They all would have bravely spoken out against slavery, and worked tirelessly against it."[1]

No, they wouldn't have. They may understandably want to send that signal now when it's safe to do so, but back then they would have likely behaved the same most everyone else did at the time.[2]

Lemmings Rarely Make History

The social default makes us fear being snubbed, ridiculed, and treated like an idiot. In most people's minds, this fear of losing social capital outweighs any potential upsides of deviating from the social norm and disposes them to accept it.[3]

Fear holds us back from taking risks and reaching our potential.

No one grows up saying I want to do the same thing everyone else is doing. And yet there is a comfort to surrounding yourself with people who agree with you, or who are doing the same thing you're doing. So while there is sometimes embedded wisdom in the crowd, mistaking the comfort of the collective for evidence that what you're doing is going to lead to better results is the social default's big lie.

The only way to outperform if you're doing undifferentiated work is to work harder than everyone else. Imagine a team of ditchdiggers working with their hands. A slight variation in the amount of soil moved per hour is barely perceptible. Your work is indistinguishable from that of the person next to you. The only way to move more dirt is to dig for longer. Within this paradigm, the ditchdigger who takes a week off to experiment and invent the shovel seems crazy. Not only do they look like a fool for taking a risk, but their cumulative production falls behind for every day they are not digging. Only when the shovel comes along do others see its advantage. Success requires shamelessness. So too does failure.

Doing something different means you might underperform, but it also means you might change the game entirely.

If you do what everyone else does, you'll get the same results that everyone else gets.* Best practices aren't always the best. By definition, they're average.

If you don't know enough about what you're doing to make your own decisions, you probably should do what everyone is doing. If you want better-than-average results, though, you'll have to think clearly. And thinking clearly is thinking independently. Sometimes you have to break free of the social default and do something differently from those around you. Fair warning: it's going to get uncomfortable.

Our desire to fit in often overpowers our desire for a better outcome. Instead of trying something new, we tell ourselves something new.

Deviating from established practices can be painful. Who wants to try something different that might not work? We could end up losing people's respect, their friendship, and even our job if we deviate too far from the status quo without producing the right results. This is why we rarely try new approaches, and when we do, we often proceed with so much trepidation that the smallest setback sends us back to the safety blanket of conformity.

It's easy to take comfort in the fact that other people agree with us. As legendary investor Warren Buffett pointed out, though, "The fact that other people agree or disagree with you makes you neither right nor wrong. You will be right if your facts and reasoning are correct."

The people executing established practices say they want new ideas, but they just don't want the bad ones. And because they so want to avoid the bad ones, they never deviate enough to find new good ones.

---

* Peter Kaufman reminds me of this all the time.

While we need divergence from the norm to make progress, not all divergence is advantageous. To be successful, it's not enough to do something different; you also need to be right. To do something different, you need to think different. And that means you will stand out.*

Lou Brock might have put it best when he said, "Show me a guy who's afraid to look bad, and I'll show you a guy you can beat every time." In other words, someone who's possessed by the social default is easy to defeat.

Warren Buffett similarly highlighted the effects of the social default in his 1984 letter to Berkshire Hathaway's shareholders:

> Most managers have very little incentive to make the intelligent-but-with-some-chance-of-looking-like-an-idiot decision. Their personal gain/loss ratio is all too obvious: if an unconventional decision works out well, they get a pat on the back and, if it works out poorly, they get a pink slip. (Failing conventionally is the route to go; as a group, lemmings may have a rotten image, but no individual lemming has ever received bad press.)[4]

Lemmings might make small changes, sure, but not the changes they need in order to make an outsize impact. While they'll talk

---

* Most people are chasing complexity. They learn the basics enough to be average, then look for the secret, shortcut, or hidden knowledge. Mastering the basics is the key to being ruthlessly effective. The basics might seem simple but that doesn't mean they're simplistic. The best in the world probably don't have some secret shortcut or hidden knowledge. They merely understand the fundamentals better than others. My favorite example of this is Warren Buffett's saying "The first rule of investing is to never lose money." Despite the lifetime of wisdom behind it, people dismiss it as too simple. An exercise in thinking comes from reasoning your way to this insight through first principles from the ground up.

about how they're doing great things to change the course of events, when you dig beneath the surface, things are the same as before. What's really changed is the marketing.

Change happens only when you're willing to think independently, when you do what nobody else is doing, and risk looking like a fool because of it. Once you realize you've been doing what everyone else is doing—and only because they're already doing it—it's time to try something new.

Later I'll discuss more examples of how the social default operates and how to combat it. For the time being keep the following in mind: if you find yourself exerting energy to fit in with a crowd, if you're frequently fearful of disappointing other people, if you're afraid of being an outsider, or if the threat of scorn fills you with dread, then beware! The social default is in charge.

The Inertia Default

The great enemy of any attempt to change men's habits is inertia. Civilization is limited by inertia.

—EDWARD L. BERNAYS,
Propaganda

IN THE MID-2000S, I INVESTED A SIGNIFICANT PORTION of my net worth into a small restaurant chain. A large investor had bought a controlling stake in the company and managed to turn around the operations, but those changes weren't yet reflected in the company's stock price. The CEO said and did all the right things. It was a compelling opportunity, so I went all in.

Over the subsequent years, however, the CEO's attitude changed. What began as a fair partnership turned into a dictatorship. Like a pot of water coming to boil, the change was slow and hard to notice until, all of a sudden, it was boiling over.

I'd made multiples on the investment and believed in its

future, so I was hesitant to exit the position too quickly—but eventually the facts became overwhelming, and I had to sell. After a bit of success, the ego default had taken control of the CEO. Suddenly all partners weren't exactly equal, one was better than the rest.*

Changing my mind took a while. Each transgression by the CEO was minor and easy to explain away. It was only after I'd stepped away from the situation and began viewing it with some perspective that I realized how far the behavior had gone. I was lucky to get out before it became apparent to everyone else—I came awfully close to losing a whole lot of money.†

The inertia default pushes us to maintain the status quo. Starting something is hard but so too is stopping something.[1] We resist change even when change is for the best.

The Latin word *inertia* means literally "inertness": that is, laziness or idleness. In physics, "inertia" refers to an object resisting a change in its state of motion. Hence, a popular way of stating Newton's first law of motion—the law of inertia—is this: "A body in motion tends to stay in motion, and a body at rest tends to stay at rest."

Objects never change if they're left alone. They don't start moving on their own, nor do they stop moving till something stops them.‡ This law of physics can also be applied to human behavior and our instinct to resist even beneficial change. The physicist Leonard Mlodinow sums it up this way: "Once our

---

* Hierarchy is a powerful biological instinct.

† At the time of this writing, the company's stock price has had a negative return over the past ten years, a period of massive returns of the stock market in general. There is no doubt some luck involved in my selling at the top.

‡ Some fifty years before Newton published his formulation of the law, Descartes summed it up like this: "Each thing, as far as is in its power, always remains in the same state; and that consequently, when it is once moved, it always continues to move."

minds are set in a direction, they tend to continue in that direction unless acted upon by some outside force."[2] This cognitive inertia is why changing our minds is hard.

Inertia keeps us in jobs we hate and in relationships that don't make us happy, because in both cases we know what to expect and it's comforting to have our expectations reliably met.

One reason we resist change is that keeping things the way they are requires almost no effort. This helps explain why we get complacent. It takes a lot of effort to build momentum but far less to maintain it. Once something becomes "good enough," we can stop the effort and still get decent results. The inertia default leverages our desire to stay in our comfort zone, relying on old techniques or standards even when they're no longer optimal.

Another reason we tend to push back against change is that doing something different might lead to worse results. There is an asymmetry to change—we take negative results to heart more than positive ones. Worse results make us stand out for the wrong reasons. Why risk looking like an idiot when you can remain average? We'd rather be average than risk the possibility of landing somewhere below average.

Inertia is evident in many of our daily habits, such as when we stick to the same grocery store brand even if a new, superior one appears on the market. This reluctance to try new products is often due to the uncertainty and effort involved in evaluating them. To combat this, companies often offer free samples to customers, which serves as a low-risk way for them to try a new product and evaluate its quality without the fear of disappointment.

We like to think we're open-minded and willing to change our beliefs when the facts change, but history has shown otherwise. When the automobile was first introduced, many critics dismissed it as a mere fad, arguing that horses and carriages were a more reliable mode of transportation. Similarly, when the airplane was first invented, people were skeptical of its practicality and safety. The radio, television, and internet all faced similar initial skepticism, yet despite this, each of these inventions has had a profound impact on the way we live today.

The "zone of average" is a dangerous place when it comes to inertia. It's the point where things are working well enough that we don't feel the need to make any changes. We hope things will magically improve. Of course, they rarely do. For example, staying in a relationship that is too good to leave and too bad to stay is a perfect example of the zone of average. If things were much worse, we would act, but since they're not terrible, we stay, and hope things get better.

Doubling Down When You're Wrong

As the famous quote often falsely attributed to Charles Darwin goes, "It's not the strongest of the species that survives, nor the most intelligent that survives. It is the one that is most adaptable to change."[3] Even though it's a misquotation, it's not useless just because it's not Darwin.

When circumstances change, we need to adapt. But inertia closes minds and stifles the motivation to change how we've been doing things. It makes it harder to imagine alternative methods, and discourages experimentation and course correction.

For instance, public statements can create inertia. Putting something on the record establishes expectations along with social pressure to meet those expectations. When new information challenges one of our statements, we might instinctively dismiss it and emphasize the old information that supported it. We want to be consistent with what we said. Changing our minds becomes increasingly difficult. We witness how, say, people label a politician a "flip-flopper" instead of "intelligent" when they change their position in response to the facts, and our fear of the social implications of changing our minds continues to grow.

Inertia also prevents us from doing hard things. The longer we avoid the hard thing we know we should do, the harder it becomes to do. Avoiding conflict is comfortable and easy. The longer we avoid the conflict, however, the more necessary it becomes to continue avoiding it. What starts out as avoiding a small but difficult conversation quickly grows into avoiding a large and seemingly impossible one. The weight of what we avoid eventually affects our relationship.

Groups create inertia of their own. They tend to value consistency over effectiveness, and reward people for maintaining the status quo. Inertia makes deviating from group norms difficult. The threat of standing out in a negative way too often keeps people in line. As a result, group dynamics end up favoring people who don't deviate from the defaults.

Group inertia is partly responsible for why a friend of mine, and I suspect a host of others, got married in the first place. According to him, in hindsight, "All the signs were there that it might not work out, but it seemed like a lot to start over with someone new, and everyone around us was getting engaged, so that's what we did."

The influence of inertia isn't just troubling in our work and relationships, it can also be bad for our health. In 1910, America's leading expert on industrial toxicology, Alice Hamilton, was appointed to head a survey on industrial illness in the state of Illinois. Over the next few years, she provided definitive evidence of the dangers of lead exposure in the workplace and of lead-tainted exhaust fumes from automobiles. But despite the evidence, General Motors and other car manufacturers continued producing lead-fueled vehicles. It wasn't until the 1980s that the US finally banned leaded fuel. Even today, lead continues to be used for other applications, despite the availability of nontoxic options at a similar price.[4]

Inertia keeps us doing things that don't get us what we want. It operates in our subconscious largely undetected until its effects are too hard to counter. Later I'll discuss more examples of the inertia default at work and how to combat it. For the time being keep the following in mind: if you find yourself biting your tongue in group situations, if you find yourself or your team resisting change or continuing to do something in one way simply because that's how you've always done it in the past—be on your guard! The inertia default is likely at work.

Default to Clarity

A man can do as he wills, but not will as he wills.

—ARTHUR SCHOPENHAUER

WHILE WE CAN'T ELIMINATE OUR DEFAULTS, WE CAN RE-
program them. If we want to improve our behavior, accomplish
more of our goals, and experience greater joy and meaning in
our lives, we need to learn to manage our defaults.

The good news is that the same biological tendencies that
make us react without reasoning can be reprogrammed into
forces for good.

Think of your default patterns of thinking, feeling, and
acting as algorithms you've been programmed to run unconsciously in response to inputs from other people or the environment. We don't think about moving our knee when the doctor
hits it with a reflex hammer. It just moves. The same thing happens with your thoughts and actions. We receive some type of
input from the world and then execute an algorithm that processes that input and automatically produces an output.

Many of the algorithms you're running have been programmed into you by evolution, culture, ritual, your parents, and your community. Some of these algorithms help move you closer to what you want; others move you further away.

You unconsciously adopt the habits of the people you spend time with, and those people make it easier or harder for you to achieve progress toward what you want to achieve. The more time you spend with people, the more likely you start to think and act as they do.

Eventually, almost everyone loses the battle with willpower; it's only a matter of time. Consider my parents. Neither of them smoked when they joined the armed forces, but it didn't take long for them to follow the lead of their smoking coworkers. At first, they resisted, but as the days turned into weeks, the grind of constantly saying no wore them down. Decades later, quitting proved nearly impossible because everyone around them smoked. The very same force that encouraged them to start was now preventing them from stopping. They were only able to kick their habit when they changed their environment. They had to find new friends whose default behavior was their desired behavior.

That's just how it goes sometimes when we're forming or breaking habits. What may look like discipline often involves a carefully created environment to encourage certain behaviors. And what may look like poor choices is often just someone trying their best to use willpower and bumping up against their defaults. The people with the best defaults are typically the ones with the best environment. Sometimes it's part of a deliberate strategy, and sometimes it's just plain luck. Either way, it's easier to align yourself with the right behavior when everyone else is already doing it.

The way to improve your defaults isn't by willpower but by

creating an intentional environment where your desired behavior becomes the default behavior.

Joining groups whose default behaviors are your desired behavior is an effective way to create an intentional environment. If you want to read more, join a book club. If you want to run more, join a running club. If you want to exercise more, hire a trainer. Your chosen environment, rather than your willpower alone, will help nudge you toward the best choices.

It's easier said than done, though. Reprogramming a computer is simply a matter of rewriting lines of code, while reprogramming yourself is a longer and more involved process. It's this process that I describe in the chapters that follow.

PART 2

BUILDING STRENGTH

*Criticizing others is easier than
coming to know yourself.*

—BRUCE LEE

COUNTERACTING THE ENEMIES of clear thinking
requires more than willpower.

Our defaults work off deeply ingrained biological
tendencies—our tendencies for self-preservation, for
recognizing and maintaining social hierarchies, and for
defending ourselves and our territory. We can't simply
know these tendencies exist and then will them out of
existence. On the contrary, the feeling that willpower is
all it takes to remove these forces is one of the tricks
they use to keep us under their control.

To stop our defaults from impeding good judgment,
we need to harness equally powerful biological forces.
We need to take the same forces that the defaults would

use to ruin us and turn them to our advantage. Chief among them is the force of inertia.

Inertia is a double-edged sword. We saw earlier that inertia is a tendency to maintain the status quo. If the status quo is sub-optimal or dysfunctional, inertia works against us. But the status quo doesn't have to be sub-optimal. If you train yourself to consistently think, feel, and act in ways that further your most important goals—if, in other words, you *build strength*—then inertia becomes a nearly unstoppable force that unlocks your potential.

Establishing rituals is the key to creating positive inertia. Rituals focus the mind on something other than the moment. They can be as simple as taking a quick pause before responding to someone's point of contention at work. One of my old mentors used to tell me, "When someone slights you in a meeting, take a deep breath before you speak and watch how often you change what you're about to say."

Rituals are hidden in plain sight anywhere temperament matters for performance. The next time you watch a basketball game or tennis match, notice how the players always bounce the ball the same number of times before shooting a free throw or serving. It doesn't matter if the previous play was the best or worst of your career. Rituals force the mind to focus on the next play, not the last one.

Strength is the power to press pause on your defaults and exercise good judgment. It doesn't matter what's going on in the world, or how unfair things may seem. It doesn't matter that you feel embarrassed, threatened, or angry. The person who can take a step back for a second, center themselves, and get out of the moment will outperform the person who can't.

When Rudyard Kipling wrote his classic poem "If—" the one that goes, "If you can keep your head when all about you / Are losing theirs and blaming it on you, / If you can trust yourself when all . . . doubt you"—he made a convincing case for personal strength.*

Building strength is about domesticating the wild horses of our nature—training and harnessing them to improve our lives. It's about turning the headwinds of our biology into tailwinds that carry us reliably toward our most cherished goals.

Here are four key strengths you'll need:

Self-accountability: holding yourself accountable for developing your abilities, managing your inabilities, and using reason to govern your actions

Self-knowledge: knowing your own strengths and weaknesses—what you're capable of doing and what you're not

Self-control: mastering your fears, desires, and emotions

Self-confidence: trusting in your abilities and your value to others

I'll define each of these strengths and discuss how they counteract your defaults, before explaining how you can begin to build them and take command of your life.

●

---

* Removed the word "men" from the quote.

Self-Accountability

I am the master of my fate,
I am the captain of my soul.

—W. E. HENLEY,
"INVICTUS"

SELF-ACCOUNTABILITY MEANS TAKING RESPONSIBILITY for your abilities, your inabilities, and your actions. If you can't do that, you might never move forward.

You might not have someone in your life who holds you accountable, but that doesn't matter. You can hold yourself accountable. Others might not expect more from you, but you can expect more from yourself. No one else need reward or punish you into it.

External rewards are nice, but they're optional; you don't need them to do your best. Your honest judgments about yourself are more important than anyone else's. And when you screw up, you should be strong enough to look in the mirror and say, "This was my fault. I need to do better." While you may never have asked for it, you're in charge of your own life—and a larger part of your outcomes than you may think.

People who lack self-accountability tend to run on autopilot. This is the exact opposite of commanding your own life. These people constantly succumb to external pressure: seeking rewards, avoiding punishments, and measuring themselves against other people's scoreboards. They're followers, not leaders. They don't take responsibility for their mistakes. Instead, they always try to blame other people, circumstances, or bad luck—nothing's ever their fault.

Well, I have news for you. It's all your fault.

There is always something you can do in the moment today to better your position tomorrow. You might not be able to solve the problem, but your next action will make the situation better or worse. There is always an action you can control, however tiny, that helps you achieve progress.

Excuses, Excuses

Complaining is not a strategy. You have to work with the world as you find it, not as you would have it be.

—JEFF BEZOS[1]

One Sunday morning early in my career, I arrived at work to find a colleague of mine already there. We were working on a critical piece of software for an upcoming covert operation. He approached me shortly after I sat down at my desk.

"That code you were writing was supposed to be done two days ago," he said. "The operation is tonight, and we can't go without you. We still have to test. You've put the whole thing in jeopardy. People are relying on us."

In the post-9/11 world, we were all working nonstop and

were under a lot of pressure. No one was sleeping more than five or six hours a night. Our health was questionable as we injected ourselves with coffee and Jolt cola once or twice an hour.

We were writing complex, mission-critical software at the lowest levels of the operating system—difficult stuff even in the best of circumstances. There was no manual for this stuff, and you couldn't simply Google how to do it.

We were breaking new ground. The time pressure didn't help. We were doing all we could, yet it never seemed like enough. And after years of sixty-hour workweeks and constant pressure, our personal and professional relationships were strained and starting to crack.

My response felt completely natural: "But . . . I had all of these meetings and got pulled into this other project the director said was top priority. And . . . I planned to work on it Friday morning, but the bus got stuck in the snow, and it took two hours to get to work."

I thought I kept my composure pretty well, but my inner dialogue was even more defensive. It went something like this: "Dude! Cut me some slack. It's Sunday. I haven't had a vacation in years. I spend way more time with you than with my girlfriend. I'm doing the best I can, and nothing I do ever seems to be enough."

"So, you're telling me this wasn't your fault?" he said innocently, setting a trap I didn't see.

"Look, a lot of stuff came up that I couldn't control," I said. "Don't worry. I'll get it done today."

"That's bullshit! It is your fault. Stop making excuses." He turned his back and started walking away. "Do what needs to be done, or we'll have to call off the operation because of you," he said without a backward glance.

I suddenly felt energized, and not with the positive energy of surging toward a goal. The defaults took control. This was ego-defending energy. I was defending my territory, defending my very sense of self.

There's no greater source of renewable energy in the world than when you're defending your own self-image. While my colleague didn't threaten me physically, he threatened how I saw myself as working hard and getting things done. And when someone threatens how you see yourself, you stop thinking and start reacting.

I began writing up a list of all the things I'd done that week—how many hours I'd worked, how many projects I'd worked on, how many people and operations I'd helped. As I rehearsed these points, I got angrier and angrier. The inertia of my negative emotions turned into a powerful doom loop. I wasn't conscious of the path I was on. I was reacting, not reasoning. My power to make excuses felt limitless: "Who is this guy to tell me it's my fault?! He doesn't see what I see!"

I emailed him the list. It filled over a page. His response arrived a few moments later:

> **I don't care. It's your responsibility to our team and our mission to get your shit done. If you can't own that, learn from it, and figure it out for next time. I don't want to work with you.**
>
> **PS Don't blame the bus for being late. Buy a car.**

WTF!?!! My response moved beyond mental and became physical. My heart rate increased, and my eyes narrowed as I lost control of my feelings and thoughts. That short email derailed me for a few hours.

All the energy we put into defending ourselves comes at the expense of the very thing that would make the situation better: moving on and doing what needs to be done. It's a choice we don't realize we're making. Had someone tapped me on the shoulder and said, "You're about to spend three hours of energy on this, are you sure you want to do that?" I would have said no.

While that email was neither nice nor fair, it was kind and it changed my life. Sure, my colleague could've been gentler.* But that didn't mean he was wrong.

Too often, the people we ask for feedback are nice but not kind. Kind people will tell you things a nice person will not. A kind person will tell you that you have spinach on your teeth. A nice person won't because it's uncomfortable. A kind person will tell us what holds us back, even when it's uncomfortable. A nice person avoids giving us critical feedback because they're worried about hurting our feelings. No wonder we think other people will be interested in our excuses.†

My team was unmoved by the fact that the bus was late and it wasn't my fault. All that mattered was the success of the operation. And results are what it usually boils down to.

No one cares about your excuses as much as you do. In fact, no one cares about your excuses at all, except you.

---

* He would go on to become my best friend.
† Sarah Jones Simmer taught me the difference between kind and nice on episode 135 of *The Knowledge Project* podcast.

No One Cares. It's Your Fault

When people's actions have outcomes that don't line up with how they see themselves, they tend to insulate their egos by blaming other people or unfavorable circumstances. Psychologists even have a term for this tendency. They call it *self-serving bias*, a habit of evaluating things in ways that protect or enhance our self-image. Statements like "It was a great idea just poorly executed," "We did the best we could," and "We never should've been in this situation in the first place" are often manifestations of this bias.*

Here's the thing: It might be true. Maybe it really wasn't a bad idea, just bad execution. Maybe you really did do the best you could. Maybe you never should have been in that situation in the first place. Unfortunately, it doesn't matter. No one cares. None of it changes the outcome or solves the problems that still remain.

Not Your Fault? It's Still Your Responsibility

Just because something happened that was outside of your control doesn't mean it's not your responsibility to deal with it the best you can.

Our desire to protect ourselves prevents us from moving forward. It's tempting to absolve yourself, throwing your hands up and claiming you have no control over the situation you've landed in. And sure, sometimes that's true. There are circumstances of chance that have a negative impact. People suffer

---

* Self-serving bias is also self-preserving. The self we're preserving is our very sense of self—our identity.

misfortune all the time for reasons beyond their control: stray bullets, diseases, getting struck by a drunk driver.

Complaining does nothing to change the present situation you find yourself in, though. Thinking about how it wasn't your fault doesn't make anything better. The consequences are still yours to deal with.

Always focus on the next move, the one that gets you closer or further from where you want to go.

If you play poker, you learn this intuitively. You're dealt a hand based mostly on luck. Feeling sorry for yourself, complaining about the hand you were dealt, or blaming others for how they played their hands only distracts you from what you can control. Your responsibility is to play the hand as best you can.

You can put energy into things you control or things you don't control. All the energy you put toward things you don't control comes out of the energy you can put toward the things you can.

While no one chooses difficult circumstances, adversity provides opportunity. It allows us to test ourselves, and see who we've become. The test isn't against other people, though; it's against our former selves. Are we better than we were yesterday? When circumstances are easy, it's hard to distinguish ordinary people from extraordinary ones, or to see the extraordinary within ourselves. As the Roman slave Publilius Syrus once said, "Anyone can steer the ship when the sea is calm."*

The path to being exceptional begins when you decide to be responsible for your actions no matter the situation. Exceptional people know they can't change the hand they've been

---

* *The Moral Sayings of Publilius Syrus*, 358. I named my investment company Syrus Partners (syruspartners.com) after him.

dealt, and don't waste time wishing for a better one. They focus instead on how they're going to play the cards they have to achieve the best result. They don't hide behind others. The best people rise to the challenge—whatever it is. They choose to live up to their best self-image instead of surrendering to their defaults.

One of the most common mistakes people make is bargaining with how the world should work instead of accepting how it does work. Anytime you find yourself or your colleagues complaining "that's not right," or "that's not fair," or "it shouldn't be that way," you're bargaining, not accepting. You want the world to work in a way that it doesn't.

Failing to accept how the world really works puts your time and energy toward proving how right you are. When the desired results don't materialize, it's easy to blame circumstances or others. I call this the wrong side of right. You're focused on your ego not the outcome.

Solutions appear when you stop bargaining and start accepting the reality of the situation. That's because focusing on the next move, rather than how you got here in the first place, opens you up to a lot of possibilities. When you put outcome over ego, you get better results.

How You Respond Can Always Make Things Better or Worse

You can't control everything, but you can control your response, which makes circumstances better or worse. Each response has an impact on the future, taking you either a step closer to or a step further from the outcomes you want and the person you want to be.

One effective question to ask yourself before you act is,

"Will this action make the future easier or harder?"* This surprisingly simple question helps change your perspective on the situation and avoid making things worse. As my grandfather (and many others) used to say, "If you find yourself in a hole, the first thing you need to do is stop digging."

One day in my mid-twenties, I found myself in my mentor's office. I had missed out on a promotion—the first one I'd been up for and failed to get—and I was complaining to him about how unfair it was.

"Why is this happening to me?" I remember saying. "Is someone trying to send me a message?" I started talking trash about the person who'd made the decision, when my mentor cut me off.

"You're refusing to accept something that already happened," he said. "And that's crazy."

"Crazy?" I replied.

"Yes. It's already happened. You can't argue with it."

"Listen," he continued, "it really sucks. You're more than qualified. But you didn't get it, and there is a reason you didn't get it. The key here is to stop blaming others and take ownership."

I let his point sink in. He was right. The world didn't just *happen* to me. It wasn't out to get me. I needed to look inside myself, honestly assess what I'd contributed to this outcome, and update my way of doing things.

As I left my mentor's office, the implication was clear. If I couldn't learn self-accountability, I wasn't going to go very far.

---

*I use a version of this on my kids. "Is this behavior moving you closer to what you want or further away?" It's amazingly effective.

Complaining Is Not a Solution

Facing reality is hard. It's much easier to blame things we have no control over than look for our own contributions.

Too often we fight against the feedback the world gives us, to protect our beliefs. Rather than changing ourselves, we want the world to change. And if we don't have the power to change it, we do the only thing we feel we can do: complain.

Complaining isn't productive. It only misleads you into thinking that the world should function in a way that it doesn't. Distancing yourself from reality makes it harder to solve the problems you face. There is always something you can do today to make the future easier, though, and the moment you stop complaining is the moment you start finding it.

You Are Not a Victim

The most important story is the one you tell yourself. While telling yourself a positive story doesn't ensure a good outcome, telling yourself a negative story often guarantees a bad one.

Each of us is the hero of the story we tell ourselves about ourselves. Being at fault when things go wrong doesn't suit the hero status we ascribe to ourselves. So, when it comes to explaining why things went wrong, we look for someone else to blame.

While pointing fingers when we don't get the results we want might satisfy us in the moment, it doesn't give us better judgment, and it doesn't make us better people. It's instead a defensive reaction prompted by our ego default—a reaction that keeps us nestled in the arms of weakness and fragility.

When you constantly blame circumstances, the environment, or other people, you are effectively claiming that you had little ability to affect the outcome. But that's not what actually happened. The truth is that we make repeated choices in life that become habits, those habits determine our paths, and those paths determine our outcomes. When we explain away those unwanted outcomes, we absolve ourselves of any responsibility for producing them.

There's a word for people who always respond to problems by blaming others or circumstances: *victims*. Of course, they're often not actually victims. They just feel like they are, and that feeling gets in the way of good judgment. Chronic victims feel helpless, powerless, and often hopeless. Nothing is ever their fault; it is always someone or something else that got in the way. No one begins life wanting to be a chronic victim, but the slow accumulation of responses that avoid responsibility makes it hard for people to see that's what they're becoming. Eventually, it's just who they are.

There are points in the process of becoming a chronic victim when people realize they're lying to themselves. They realize the story they're telling themselves isn't quite true. They know they're responsible. But facing reality and taking responsibility is hard. It's uncomfortable. It's so much easier to hide and to blame other people, circumstances, or luck.

Ironically, the people who care the most about chronic victims often unintentionally encourage their blame game. When things don't go our way, it's natural to vent to family members or close friends. They're loving and supportive and have the best intentions for us. They would love to validate our interpretation of the situation, and offer us relief. But when they do that, nothing has changed. Our incorrect view of the world remains intact. They don't encourage us to re-evaluate our patterns of thinking, feeling, and acting. And if we're thrust into similar circumstances later on, we'll likely respond the same way and get the same disappointing results.

On the other hand, have you ever had a friend tell you, "You messed up pretty bad there. How can I help you make this right?" or "Let me tell you the one thing I think is holding you back from getting the results you want"?

If you have a friend like that, call them now and thank them. Their presence in your life is a rare gift. Cherish it!

Or perhaps one of your parents has done that for you. When I was thirteen years old, I was standing with a group of my friends after school. They were teasing one of our classmates and I was watching. The teachers intervened before things got out of control, and it ended as quickly as it began. I didn't realize, however, that my father was parked nearby, watching. When I got in the car, he asked me what had happened.

"Nothing," I said. My father looked at me with that parental look I now give my own kids. "We were just giving the guy a bit of a hard time," I said.

"Why?" he asked.

"Everyone was doing it. It wasn't serious. Relax."

He stopped the car in the middle of the road, and gave me that look again.

"You chose to be there, and you chose not to stop it," he said. "You can't do stuff just because everyone else is doing it and expect to get a free pass. You're responsible for your choices. You're better than you were in that moment."

Then he didn't say another word to me until the next day.

The lesson was an important one: the things you choose not to do often matter as much as the things you choose to do. The real test of a person is the degree to which they are willing to nonconform to do the right thing.

It took a while for me to realize that he was more disappointed in me for not stopping the others than for being there in the first place.[2] He didn't want me to become a passive person—the kind of person whose behavior is dictated by the people and events around him. He didn't want me to become a chronic victim of circumstances.

No successful person wants to work with a chronic victim. The only people who want to work with victims are other victims.

If you pay attention to chronic victims, you'll notice how fragile they are—how dependent their attitudes and feelings are on things they don't control. When things go their way, they're happy; when things don't, they're defensive, passive-aggressive, and occasionally *aggressive*-aggressive. If their spouse is in a bad mood, they're in a bad mood too. If they hit traffic on the way to work, they bring their anger and frustration to work with them. If a project they're leading isn't on track, they blame someone on their team.

Self-accountability is the strength of realizing that even though you don't control everything, you do control how you respond to everything. It's a mindset that empowers you to act and not just react to whatever life throws at you. It transforms obstacles into opportunities for learning and growth. It means realizing that the way you respond to hardship matters more to your happiness than the hardship itself. And it means understanding that the best path is often just to accept things and move on.

Self-Knowledge

Know thyself.

—INSCRIPTION ON THE TEMPLE
OF APOLLO AT DELPHI

SELF-KNOWLEDGE IS ABOUT KNOWING YOUR OWN strengths and weaknesses. You must know what you can do and what you can't; your powers and limitations, your strengths and vulnerabilities, what's in your control and what isn't. You know what you know, and what you don't know. And you know, moreover, that you have cognitive blind spots—that there are things you don't know, and you don't know you don't know them—what Donald Rumsfeld famously called "unknown unknowns."

If you want to better understand your level of self-knowledge, ask yourself how many times a day you utter the phrase "I don't know." If you never say, "I don't know," you're probably dismissing things that surprise you or explaining away outcomes instead of understanding them.

Understanding what you do and don't know is the key to playing games you can win.

I witnessed a powerful display of self-knowledge recently, at a group dinner with a very successful friend who'd made a fortune in real estate. A savvy investor at the dinner pitched him on a company he was taking private. The idea was one of the most compelling I had heard in years.

After hearing out the pitch, my friend paused for a second, took a sip of water, and said, "I'm not interested in investing." The entire table sat in silence, wondering what we had missed. Someone finally broke the silence by asking him why he was passing.

"I don't know anything about that space," he said. "I like to stick to what I know."

As we left the restaurant, the conversation continued. He admitted that the pitch sounded great, he trusted the person, and thought investors would make a lot of money on the deal. (They did.) Then he told me, "The key to successful investing is to know what you know and stick to it."

My friend knew real estate well, and he knew if he played in that space and was patient, he couldn't help but be successful.

It's Not the Size of Your Knowledge, but How You Use It

Knowing just what it is that you know is among the most practical skills you can have. The size of what you know isn't nearly as important as having a sense of your knowledge's boundaries.

At dinner one night, Charlie Munger elaborated on the same idea my real estate investor friend had put forth. He said,

"When you play games where other people have the aptitude and you don't, you're going to lose. You have to figure out where you have an edge and stick to it."

It's not enough to know where you have an edge; you also have to know when you are operating outside of it. If you don't know which side of the line you're on, or that there even is a line at all, you're outside your boundaries.

Self-knowledge isn't limited just to hard skills, though. It's also about knowing when you're vulnerable to your defaults— the kinds of situations where circumstances do the thinking for you. Maybe you're prone to being overly emotional—to sadness, anger, or intrusive self-defeating thoughts. Maybe you have a short temper when you're tired, or you become an ogre when you're hungry. Maybe you're acutely sensitive to social pressure and the threat of social scorn.

Knowing about your strengths and weaknesses, your abilities and their limits is essential to counteracting your defaults. If you don't know your vulnerabilities, your defaults will exploit them to gain control of your circumstances.

Self-Control

Give me that man
That is not passion's slave, and I will wear him
In my heart's core, ay, in my heart of heart.

—WILLIAM SHAKESPEARE,
Hamlet

SELF-CONTROL IS THE ABILITY TO MASTER YOUR FEARS, desires, and other emotions.

Emotions are an inescapable part of human life. Mammals like us evolved to respond quickly to immediate environmental threats and opportunities—fear in response to a threat, enjoyment in response to a social-bonding experience, sadness in response to a loss. We can't eliminate these physiological reactions or the conditions that trigger them. We can only manage how we respond to them.

Some people are like corks bobbing around in the waves of an emotional sea. Their actions are in thrall to their emotions: anger, joy, sadness, fear—whatever gets triggered in the moment. Other people, however, decide to take command of their life. They seize the helm, decide where they want to go, and steer the ship in that direction despite the waves. They still experience ups and downs like everybody else; they just don't allow those waves of emotion to determine the direction of their life. Instead, they turn the wheel as needed using good judgment to keep themselves on course.

Self-control is about creating space for reason instead of just blindly following instincts. It's about being able to view and manage your emotions as if they were inanimate objects—things that don't have the power to determine what you do unless you let them. It's about putting distance between yourself and your emotions, and realizing that you have the power to determine how you respond to them. You can react when they prompt you, or instead think clearly and consider whether they're worth following.

The emotion default tries to remove any distance between you and your emotions, triggering a reaction in the absence of any deliberation. It wants to win the present moment, even if it means sabotaging the future. Self-control empowers you to keep emotion in check, though.

If you've ever seen a toddler throw a tantrum, you've seen what the emotion default can do with someone who hasn't learned self-control. What's truly frightening is that some adults are only marginally better than a toddler at fending it off. These are people who lack self-control and are routinely carried away by their emotions.

A large part of achieving success is having the self-control to do whatever needs to be done, regardless of whether you feel like doing it at the moment. Emotional intensity is far less important in the long run than disciplined consistency. Inspiration and excitement might get you going, but persistence and routine are what keep you going until you reach your goals. Anyone can maintain excitement for a few minutes, but the longer a project takes, the fewer the people who can maintain their excitement for it. The most successful people have the self-control to keep going anyway. It's not always exciting, but they still show up.

Self-Confidence

SELF-CONFIDENCE IS ABOUT TRUSTING IN YOUR ABILITIES and your value to others.

You need self-confidence to think independently and to stand firm in the face of social pressure, ego, inertia, or emotion. You need it to understand that not all results are immediate, and to focus on doing what it takes to earn them eventually.

Children develop self-confidence when they learn simple skills like pulling up a zipper, tying their shoes, or riding a bike. Eventually, that self-confidence evolves and propels them to develop more complex abilities as adults—for instance, writing software, painting murals, or cheering up a disheartened friend.

Self-confidence empowers resilience in the aftermath of negative feedback, and adaptability in the face of changing circumstances. You know what your abilities are and how they add value, whether other people appreciate them or not. If you've forged a healthy sense of self-confidence, it will see you through whatever emerging challenges and difficulties come your way.

Confidence vs. Ego

Self-confidence is what empowers you to execute difficult decisions and develop self-knowledge. While the ego tries to prevent you from acknowledging any deficiencies you may have, self-confidence gives you the strength to acknowledge those deficiencies. This is how you learn humility.

Confidence without humility is generally the same thing as overconfidence—a weakness, not a strength. Confident people have the strength to admit weaknesses and vulnerabilities, to acknowledge that other people might be better at something than they are, and to ask when they need help.

It's only human to have doubts about whether you are up to a given task. Even the most capable people have doubts about this from time to time. But those who have self-confidence never give in to feelings of despair or worthlessness. That's just another ego trap. Instead, confident people stay focused on completing the task at hand, even if it involves relying on the help of others to do so. Every successful task only further serves to deepen your trust in yourself, and that's how confidence is earned.

Confidence also Comes from How You Talk to Yourself

More dreams die from a lack of confidence than a lack of competence. But while confidence is often a byproduct of our accomplishments, it also comes from how you talk to yourself.

That little voice in your head may whisper its doubts, but it should also remind you of the many hardships and challenges you've overcome in the past and the fact that you persevered. No matter who you are, you've given that little voice many positive moments to speak of. You learned to walk, despite falling down thousands of times. Maybe you failed a test at first, but then figured out what went wrong, and nailed it the next time. Perhaps you were fired, but moved on and ended up in a better position as a result. Maybe your relationship ended or your business failed or you were scared the first time you put on skis—whatever it was, you overcame it, moved past it, and you're stronger as a result.

It's important to talk to yourself about the adversity you've faced, because past hardship is where you get the confidence to face future hardship.

When I took my youngest son cliff jumping, we faced a serious dilemma. After reaching the top and looking down at the twenty-five-foot drop, he got scared and wanted to climb back down. That wasn't possible, however, because the climb down was far more dangerous than the jump—one small error and he would have landed on a bed of sharp rocks. The more he looked down, the more nervous he became. I had to do something to help him help himself out of this situation.

The first thing we did was to focus on our breathing. Your breath is a powerful tool that helps you calm your mind. We started taking a normal inhale and then immediately inhaling again with a smaller breath. It's the same way we naturally breathe when we're sobbing, and the results are similarly soothing. Only once we had relaxed our physical bodies could we change our inner dialogue.

I asked him how he was talking to himself at that moment—and it wasn't good. He was beating himself up, telling himself how dumb it had been to climb up in the first place, how he should have known better, and how scared he was. This is the same way we all tend to talk to ourselves sometimes—or at least it is in my experience.

The second thing we did was change the conversation he was having inside his head. We know how the words we say to other people impact how they feel, but we rarely think of how the words we say to ourselves impact us. I asked him to list off some of the things he'd already done that he had feared before doing them. The question was barely out of my mouth when he started to tell me about snowboarding and the time we "mistakenly" ended up on a double black diamond and the first time he went wakeboarding. The list went on. There was no shortage of situations he'd been in that had required courage.

Once he realized he had done difficult things before for the first time, he went back to focusing on his breathing. Then he jumped. Within seconds, he emerged from the water, and I could see his huge smile as he climbed back up for round two.

People who are confident aren't afraid of facing reality because they know they can handle it. Confident people don't care what other people think about them, aren't afraid of standing out, and are willing to risk looking like an idiot while they try something new. They've been beaten down and rebuilt themselves enough times to know that they can do it again if they have to. Crucially, they also know that to outperform the crowd, you have to do things differently sometimes, and that hecklers and naysayers inevitably tend to follow. They take their feedback from reality, not popular opinion.

The most important voice to listen to is the one that reminds you of all that you've accomplished in the past. And while you might not have done this particular thing before, you can figure it out.

Confidence and Honesty

Self-confidence is also the strength to accept hard truths. We all have to deal with the world as it is, not as we want it to be. The quicker you stop denying inconvenient truths and start responding to difficult realities, the better.

We all have something that we're denying right now because accepting it is hard, and we want to avoid the pain. Maybe you're in a dead-end job or you're about to go bankrupt, or you're holding an investment that you have trouble admitting didn't work out. The quicker you accept reality, though, the quicker you can deal with the implications, and the sooner you do that, the easier those implications are to manage. Most of the time, needing to wait for the right moment to do a hard thing is just an excuse: a way to rationalize putting off what needs to be done. There is no perfect moment.[1] There's only the desire to continue waiting for one.

People with self-confidence are honest about their own motivations, actions, and results. They recognize when the voice in their head might be ignoring reality. They also listen to the feedback the world gives them, instead of shopping around for other opinions.

The internet makes it easy to find people who agree with us no matter what we believe. Want to deny the Holocaust? There's a group for that. Think vaccines cause autism? Many others do as well. Heck, we *still* have a flat-earth society, whose membership spans around the globe.

You can quickly and easily be surrounded by people who share the same delusions. That doesn't make them true. Reality isn't a popularity contest. Surrounding yourself with people who tell you you're right doesn't mean you are. And once you dive into the warm water of group acceptance, it's hard to get back out. The social default strikes again!

The groups we surround ourselves with encourage us to think the problem is with the world and not with us. We think we are right and everyone else is wrong, denying reality at the expense of the energy and focus we need to adapt and improve. We do this because it feels more comfortable than accepting reality, even though it's only after we accept reality that we can attempt to change it. And we continue wondering, deep down, why we aren't getting the results we want. We wonder why some people get better results than we do, and what they're doing differently.

I was taking a stroll one day with the CEO of a large public company, when we started discussing how he hired people for key roles.

I asked, "If you could pick one trait that would predict how someone would turn out, what would it be?"

"That's easy," he said. "How willing they are to change their mind about what they think they know."

The most valuable people, he continued, weren't the ones with the best initial ideas, but the ones with the ability to quickly change their minds. They were focused on outcome over ego. By contrast, he said, the people most likely to fail were those obsessed with minute details that supported their point of view.

"They're too focused on proving they're right instead of being right," he said.

As I mentioned previously in the chapter on self-accountability, this is what I call *the wrong side of right*. It's what happens when otherwise smart people confuse the best outcome with the best outcome for them personally.[2]

In order to be right, you must be willing to change your mind. If you're not willing to change your mind, you're going to be wrong a lot. The people who frequently find themselves on the wrong side of right are people who can't zoom in and out and see the problem from multiple angles. They get locked into one perspective: their own. When you can't see a problem from multiple points of view, you have blind spots. And blind spots get you in trouble.

Admitting you're wrong isn't a sign of weakness, it's a sign of strength. Admitting that someone has a better explanation than you shows that you're adaptable. Facing reality takes courage. It takes courage to revise your ideas, or rethink something you thought you knew. It takes courage to tell yourself something is not working. It takes courage to accept feedback that bruises your self-image.

The challenge of facing reality is ultimately the challenge of facing ourselves. We must acknowledge the things we cannot control and focus our efforts to manage the things we can. Facing reality demands acknowledging our mistakes and failures, learning from them, and moving forward.

The Wrong Side of Right

Once, in New York, after I'd given a talk on making effective decisions, a woman in the audience came up to me with a question. The event had run late and I really had to get to the airport, which I apologetically informed her. In response, she offered to have her driver take me to the airport, if she could pick my brain along the way.*

---

* Nothing like a trusting Canadian to get in the car of a complete stranger in New York.

As we got into the car, she started telling me about a very difficult problem she was wrestling with. She was one of two candidates to become the next CEO of her organization and felt like the problem she was facing would make or break her chances. She walked me through the details and told me her proposed solution. Although it sounded as though her idea would indeed solve the problem, it was complicated and full of execution risk. But there was an alternative—a solution that was simpler, lower cost, and carried less risk. It was objectively a better solution. The only problem was that it was her rival's.

As she detailed some of her thinking, she spent a lot of time and effort defending herself, trying to prove her solution was the better one. She only succeeded in making it clear that she knew her own solution wasn't the best. She was on the wrong side of right. She just didn't want to admit it.

Many people feel the same way: they think they'll be worthless if they're not right. I myself used to feel the same way. Rather than let her figure out her mistake the hard way, I shared some of the harsh and expensive lessons I'd learned about that mindset and about being on the wrong side of right.

I told her that for the longest time, I thought if the best idea wasn't my idea, I'd be nothing. I thought that no one would see me as valuable, that no one would see me as insightful, that I wouldn't be contributing anything. I had my identity wrapped up in being right.

It wasn't until I began running a business that I realized how wrong I'd been. When everything is on your shoulders and the cost of being wrong is high, I told her, you tend to focus on what's right instead of who's right. The more I'd given up wanting to be right, the better the outcomes I had. I didn't care about getting the credit; I cared about getting the results.

"If you owned 100 percent of this company and couldn't

sell it for one hundred years," I asked her, "which solution would you prefer?"

There was a long pause before she answered.

"I know what I need to do," she said. "Thank you."

A few months later, my phone rang. It was her.*

"You won't believe what happened!" she said. "I got the CEO job thanks in part to your help. It was a tough pill to swallow, but I ended up supporting my rival's solution, and that's what ended up tipping the scales in my favor. When the board saw that I could put aside my ego and do what was best for the company—even if it meant supporting someone competing with me for the same role—they knew I was the right person."

Self-confidence is the strength to focus on what's right instead of who's right. It's the strength to face reality. It's the strength to admit mistakes, and the strength to change your mind. Self-confidence is what it takes to be on the right side of right.

Outcome over ego.

---

* The ability of people to get my cell number still baffles me.

Strength in Action

SELF-ACCOUNTABILITY, SELF-KNOWLEDGE, SELF-CONTROL, and self-confidence are essential to exercising good judgment. Here are a couple examples of how they work together.

Example 1: Going against the Norm

Most people who work for a three-letter agency end up staying there for their entire career. Why wouldn't you? Great salaries, a pension indexed to inflation, and a mission-focused organization full of incredibly smart and dedicated people.

When I told one of my colleagues I was quitting, they looked at me with surprise. They told me about all the risks, how I'd lose my golden pension and my benefits. They focused on what I was losing, not what I was gaining: mainly, the freedom of my time.

Leaving this job illustrates the four strengths in action. I had the self-confidence that I could figure out what came next without needing to know all the details, the self-knowledge to know that I valued time over money, the self-control to get up the next day without missing a beat, and the self-accountability to set a higher standard for performance than I ever had before.

Without self-knowledge, I never would have known what made me happy. Without self-confidence, I never would have left. Without self-accountability and self-control, I probably would have known what to work on, but I would have filled my days with easy busywork instead of the activities that moved me forward.

Example 2: Resisting the Social Default

Suppose you know from experience that you're susceptible to social pressure. On numerous occasions, for instance, you've been cajoled into buying things you didn't want from pushy salespeople, and you've agreed to take on jobs you didn't have the bandwidth for by pushy colleagues. You don't trust yourself to do better in the future using sheer willpower alone.

To protect yourself from the influence of the social default, you decide to implement a safeguard. You form a rule for yourself: never say yes to something important without thinking it over for a day.

Practicing this safeguard isn't very enjoyable. Putting someone on hold for a day might be uncomfortable in the moment, but the long-term results of implementing this safeguard are worth it. As simple as they seem, automatic rules for common situations get results. We'll explore automatic rules in the next chapter.

Implementing this plan illustrates all four of the strengths I've mentioned. Knowing your vulnerability to social pressure and the limits of your power to resist it requires self-knowledge. Deciding to do something about this vulnerability to secure better outcomes involves self-confidence. Following the rule you've made for yourself takes self-accountability. And overcoming short-term discomfort in ordinary moments for long-term gain displays self-control.*

All four of these strengths are necessary for resisting the influence of the social default. Once you have them all working together, you'll be amazed at what you can accomplish. Now let's take a look at how to build those strengths.

---

* Rules create rituals that have inertia—and in this way this rule uses the very aspect of human nature that gets us in trouble for good.

Setting the Standards

It is inevitable if you enter into relations with people on a regular basis . . . that you will grow to be like them. . . . Place an extinguished piece of coal next to a live one, and either it will cause the other one to die out, or the live one will make the other reignite. . . . Remember that if you consort with someone covered in dirt you can hardly avoid getting a little grimy yourself.

—EPICTETUS,
Discourses

THE FIRST STEP TO BUILDING ANY OF YOUR STRENGTHS IS raising the standards to which you hold yourself, a practical matter of looking around at the people and practices that pervade your day-to-day environment.

Our surroundings influence us—both our physical environment and the people around us. Few things are more important in life than avoiding the wrong people. It's tempting to think that we are strong enough to avoid adopting the worst of others, but that's not how it typically works.

We unconsciously become what we're near. If you work for a jerk, sooner or later you'll become one yourself. If your colleagues are selfish, sooner or later you become selfish. If you hang around someone who's unkind, you'll slowly become unkind. Little by little, you adopt the thoughts and feelings, the attitudes and standards of the people around you. The changes are too gradual to notice until they're too large to address.

Becoming like the people around you means that over time you come to adopt their standards. If all you see are average people, you will end up with average standards. But average standards aren't going to get you where you want to go. Standards become habits, and habits become outcomes. Few people realize that exceptional outcomes are almost always achieved by people with higher-than-average standards.

The most successful people have the highest standards, not only for others but for themselves. For instance, when I was once sent to a remote location to work, I remember standing up in a meeting to explain how some element of an operation worked. After a few moments, another person, who was widely recognized as *the* expert in this specialty, interrupted and asked me to stop talking until I knew what I was talking about. Then he got up and explained it in more detail than I thought possible. After the meeting I went to his office and talked to him. He explained that while he didn't know what it was like where I was from, the standard here was you don't speak unless you know what you're talking about.

Champions don't create the standards of excellence. The standards of excellence create champions.*

High standards are consistent across top performers. When you look at any athlete or team that performs on a level beyond what you can explain by luck or talent, you find a commitment to high standards. The New England Patriots and their coach Bill Belichick have won more games over a twenty-year span than any other NFL team. Not only that, but they also did it with a salary cap designed to level the playing field and make dynasties like theirs impossible. When all-star cornerback Darrelle Revis, who was the best in the game at his position, was a few minutes late for a practice one day, Coach Belichick sent him home immediately.[1] Belichick didn't make a big deal about it, but he was firm. Revis wouldn't be treated differently from other players. Coach didn't care what star players got away with on other teams. Revis was a New England Patriot, and he had to rise to the team's standards.

The best teachers expect more from their students and from themselves. And more often than not, the students rise to meet those expectations. The best leaders expect more from people; they hold them to the same standards they hold themselves—a higher standard than most would otherwise know is possible.

Smart People with Low Standards

The difference between average and exceptional results for a leader often comes down to whether they're consistently getting more out of smart but otherwise lazy people. I once found

---

*This was inspired by this Bill Walsh quote: "Champions behave like champions before they're champions. They have a winning standard of performance before they are winners."

myself working with one such fellow. I'd recently been promoted, and he sent me a draft asking for my "guidance and feedback." The draft was terrible and full of obvious flaws. It wasn't his best work. I knew it. And he knew it.

If you work in a large organization, I'm sure something similar has happened to you. Someone creates a half-assed draft of something that's full of poor thinking, sends it around, and waits for others to correct it. This tactic takes advantage of one of our defaults: we love correcting people. If someone does something wrong, we almost can't help but tell them how to do it the right way. So you do the work, and they get the credit in a fraction of the time it would've taken them to do it themselves. Smart. But lazy.

I didn't want to spend the rest of the evening (or my career) correcting this guy's work for him. I needed a way of changing his behavior. But how?

I remembered a story I'd read about Henry Kissinger. A staffer had drafted a memo and left it on Kissinger's desk for him to read. A while later Kissinger approached him and asked if it was his best work. The staffer said no and rewrote the entire memo. The next day the staffer ran into Kissinger again and asked what he thought. Kissinger asked him again if this was the best he could do. The staffer took the memo and rewrote it yet again. The next morning the same scenario played out, only this time the poor staffer stated that yes indeed it was his best work. Kissinger replied, "Okay, now I'll read it."

I decided to adopt Kissinger's approach. I simply replied to the email with "Is this your best work?"

The fellow responded no, asked for a few days to clarify his thinking, and came back with a version he thought was dramatically improved. Without opening the document, I shot back the same thing.

He replied, "Yes, this is the best I can do."

I read that version, and it was excellent. Now that I knew what he was capable of and he knew that I knew, I told him I expected that out of him every time. The standard was clear. I was never disappointed.

Why We Have Low Standards

Most of the time when we accept substandard work from ourselves, it's because we don't really care about it. We tell ourselves it's good enough, or the best we can manage given our time constraints. But the truth is, at least in this particular thing, we're not committed to excellence.

When we accept substandard work from others, it's for the same reason: we're not all in. When you're committed to excellence, you don't let anyone on your team half-ass it. You set the bar, you set it high, and you expect anyone working with you to work just as hard and level up to what you expect or above. Anything less is unacceptable.

When Zhang Ruimin took over as CEO at the Qingdao Refrigerator Plant, the precursor to the appliance company Haier, the company was close to failure. To send a clear signal to his new employees, Ruimin gathered them outside to witness seventy-six substandard refrigerators smashed to pieces by a sledgehammer. Ruimin kept a sledgehammer in a glass case in the boardroom for the remainder of his tenure, as a symbol of the high standard he expected from the company.[2]

Excellence Demands Excellence

Masters of their craft don't merely want to check off a box and move on. They're dedicated to what they do, and they keep at it.

Master-level work requires near fanatical standards, so masters show us what our standards should be. A master communicator wouldn't accept a ponderous, rambling email. A master programmer wouldn't accept ugly code. Neither of them would accept unclear explanations as understanding.

We'll never be exceptional at anything unless we raise our standards, both of ourselves and of what's possible. For most of us, that sounds like a lot of work. We gravitate toward being soft and complacent. We'd rather coast. That's fine. Just realize this: if you do what everyone else does, you can expect the same results that everyone else gets. If you want different results, you need to raise the bar.

Working with a master firsthand is the best education; it's the surest way of raising the bar. Their excellence demands your excellence. But most of us aren't lucky enough to have that opportunity. Still, not all is lost. If you don't have the chance to work with a master directly, you can still surround yourself with people who have higher standards by reading about them and their work.

Exemplars + Practice

THERE ARE TWO COMPONENTS TO BUILDING STRENGTH by raising the bar:

(a) Choose the right exemplars—ones that raise your standards. Exemplars can be people you work with, people you admire, or even people who lived long ago. It doesn't matter. What matters is they make you better in a certain area, like a skill, trait, or value.

(b) Practice imitating them in certain ways. Create space in the moment to reflect on what they'd do in your position, and then act accordingly.

Let's consider these components one at a time.

In the previous section, we discussed something most people never think about: if you don't curate the people in your life, the people who end up surrounding you will be there by chance and not by choice. That group includes your parents, your friends, your family, your coworkers. Sure, your high school friends might be great examples of character and acumen, but odds are they're average. Sure, your parents might be some of the smartest businesspeople in the world, but odds are they're not. It's not that you should remove these people from your life, though; controlling your environment just means intentionally adding exemplars into the mix.

Your Exemplars

Show me your role models and I'll show you your future.

When I first started working at a three-letter intelligence agency, I looked up to my colleague Matt. He was one of the best in the world at understanding how operating systems work and the various ways you can use them to your advantage. What struck me most about Matt was his incredibly high standards. Like Michael Jordan, Matt combined natural talent with a first-class work ethic. And he demanded perfection. (Is it any wonder that he was one of the best in the world?)

You couldn't say anything around Matt unless you really knew what you were talking about, or he'd correct you. He raised the bar for the entire team. Not only did he work harder than anyone else, but he consistently came up with elegant solutions to complicated problems. Matt was an exemplar: someone who modeled an exemplary way of being. He showed you what was possible.

I got lucky. Chance could've given me an average boss. Instead, it gave me Matt. The thing is, though, you don't have to rely on luck. It's possible for you to choose the people whose behavior you emulate—your exemplars—rather than merely hope you end up working with one of them.

When you choose the right exemplars—people with standards higher than yours—you can transcend the standards you've inherited from parents, friends, and acquaintances. Your exemplars show you what your standards should be. As Peter Kaufman once told me, "No technique has been more responsible for my success in life than studying and adopting the good models of others."

This wisdom has been around for a long time. In his letters to Lucilius, Seneca urges him to choose a role model or exemplar to provide a standard to live by:

> The mind should have someone whom it can respect— someone whose authority might make even its inner shrine more hallowed. . . . Happy is he who can so respect a man that the very memory of that man can calm and direct him! He who can thus respect another will quickly be respected himself. Therefore, choose a Cato, or if this seems too strict for you, choose a gentler spirit—a man like Laelius. Choose someone whose life and speech pleases you, and who displays outwardly the same character he has. Present him to yourself always as your guardian or exemplar. There is need, I insist, for someone against whom to measure our way of life; unless you have a ruler, you can't straighten what is crooked.[1]

The people we choose as our exemplars exhibit the principles, the resolve, and the overall patterns of thinking, feeling, and acting that we want to make our own. Their example helps us navigate the world. It becomes our North Star.

Most people didn't want to adopt Matt's standards because those standards were so exacting. Yet if you were willing to put in the work, Matt was a shortcut to excellence hiding in plain sight. People at the far right of the bell curve (the positive outliers) can teach you tips, tricks, and insights that might otherwise take a lifetime to learn. They've done the heavy lifting. They've already paid for the lessons, so you don't have to. Learning from and attempting to live up to Matt's standards helped me become proficient much faster than I would have become otherwise.

Look around, find the best examples you can of people with the attributes you want to cultivate—the people whose default behavior is your desired behavior, those who inspire you to raise the bar and make you want to be a better version of yourself.

Your exemplars needn't be alive. They can be either dead or fictional, as well. We can learn from both Atticus Finch and Warren Buffett, along with Genghis Khan and Batman. It's up to you.

Your Personal Board of Directors

Put all of your exemplars on your "personal board of directors," a concept that originates with author Jim Collins:

> Back in the early '80s, I made Bill [Lazier] the honorary chairman of my personal board of directors. And when I chose members . . . they were not chosen for their success. They were chosen for their values and their character. . . . They're the sorts of people I wouldn't want to let down.[2]

The exemplars on your personal board can be a mix of high accomplishment and high character. The only requirement is that they have a skill, attitude, or disposition you want to cultivate in yourself. They don't have to be perfect. All people have flaws, and your personal board will be no different. But everyone is better than us at something. Our job is to figure out what that something is and learn from it while ignoring the rest.

One of the biggest mistakes that I see people make is they don't want to learn from someone who has a character blemish or a worldview that doesn't align with theirs. Seneca captured the right approach when he said in *On the Tranquility of the Mind*, "I shall never be ashamed of citing a bad author if the line is good." Or, as Cato the Elder put it, "Be careful not to rashly refuse to learn from others."[3] Don't throw away the apple because of a bruise on the skin.

Your personal board of directors isn't static. People come and go. You're always curating the list. To take it back to *The Godfather*, sometimes you want the peacetime consigliere and sometimes you want the wartime consigliere. Sometimes you've learned what you can from someone, and you want to replace them with someone else. Each person tends to lead you to the next.

Masters have a different standard—often one of elegance and beauty. And when you put masters on your board, you raise the bar for yourself. What seemed good enough before doesn't seem good enough anymore.

One of my exemplars is Charlie Munger, the billionaire business partner of Warren Buffett. He raised my standard for holding an opinion. One night at dinner, he commented, "I never allow myself to have an opinion on anything unless I know the other side's argument better than they do."

Talk about raising the bar! Many people have opinions, but very few have done the work required to hold them. Doing that work means you can argue against yourself better than your real opponents can. It forces you to challenge your beliefs because you have to argue from both sides. It's only when you put in the work that you come to really understand an argument. You understand the reasons for and against it. Through that work you earn the confidence to endorse it.[4]

There is no better way to learn than working directly with your heroes. The benefit of working with someone in person is that it allows for a natural back-and-forth—more a coaching relationship than a mere model. A personal relationship also allows you to ask for help—to reach out when you need it. But working in person with someone you admire isn't always possible. Still, that doesn't mean you have to accept the lot of people around you.

The phone in your pocket literally gives you access to the smartest people who've ever existed, alive or dead. Even if you don't have direct contact with them, you can often listen to them talk in their own words—unfiltered! Think about that for a second. For the first time in history, you have the opportunity to listen to your exemplars explain things in their own way, without someone getting in the middle.*

If your hero is Tobi Lütke, who started Shopify, one of the most successful companies in the history of the world, you can find countless interviews with him on the internet. You can sit at the feet of the master and learn as he shares how he thinks, how he makes decisions, how he runs his company. The same goes for Peter D. Kaufman, Warren Buffett, Jeff Bezos, Tom Brady, Simone Biles, Serena Williams, or Katie Ledecky.

You can choose among the greats of history: Richard Feynman, George Washington, Charles de Gaulle, Winston Churchill, Coco Chanel, Charlie Munger, Marie Curie, Marcus Aurelius. All of them are ready to accept your invitation to be

---

* Even books are filtered by editors these days. I suppose you could make an argument that in the old days, someone could publish a book directly without a filter, but I think the point is pretty clear.

on your personal board. All you need to do is collect the best of them together and unite them in your mind. As Montaigne put it, "I have gathered a garland of other men's flowers, and nothing is mine but the cord that binds them."[5]

You're never alone if you have a personal board of directors. They're always there. You can imagine them watching you make decisions and power moves. And once you imagine them watching, your behavior is bound to reflect this new audience. They will help set the standards that you strive to live up to, and give you a ruler against which to measure yourself. You're not a failure if you come up short—if you don't write a bestselling book, or become a billionaire, or work out every day. You're not in competition with your exemplars. The only person you're competing with is the person you were yesterday. Victory is being a little better today.

Your Repository of Good Behavior

Choosing the right exemplars helps create a repository of "good behavior." As you read what people have written, as you talk to them, as you learn from their experiences, as you learn from your own experiences, you begin to build a database of situations and responses. Building this database is one of the most important things you'll ever do because it helps create space for reason in your life. Instead of reacting, and simply copying those around you, you think, "Here's what the outliers do."

When you face a new situation, you have a catalog of the responses that people on the far right of the bell curve have had in similar situations. Your baseline response moves from good to great—from reaction to reason.

Your board can pull you in the right direction despite your instincts.

If we have our board stacked with high-character people, we'll end up wanting to be the highest-character version of ourselves. We'll have the confidence to take a moral stand, and to act alone when the social tide goes the wrong way. We needn't passively follow its ebbs and flows. Our personal board gives us the courage and insight to swim in the direction that's best.

A final note on exemplars: just as other people serve on your personal board of directors, you serve on other people's boards. Denzel Washington reminds us of this point: "You never know who you touch. You never know how or when you'll have an impact, or how important your example can be to someone else."[6]

Maybe it's the new employee down the hall. Maybe it's your kids. Maybe it's your cousin. It doesn't matter. What matters is there's someone out there looking up at you and using your behavior as their North Star. Everything you do has the power to change someone else's life for the better. As Seneca said, "Happy is he who can improve others not just when he is in their presence, but even when he is in their thoughts!"[7]

Practice, Practice, Practice

Strengths of character result from habit. . . . We acquire them just as we acquire skills . . . we become builders, for instance, by building, and we become harpists by playing the harp. So too we become just by doing just actions, temperate by doing temperate actions, brave by doing brave actions.

—ARISTOTLE,
  Nicomachean Ethics, Book 2, Chapter 1

It's not enough just to pick exemplars and assemble a personal board of directors. You also have to follow their example—not just once or twice, but again and again. Only then will you internalize the standards they embody, and become the kind of person you want to be.

Imitating your exemplars involves creating space in the moment to exercise reason and evaluate your thoughts, feelings, and possible courses of action. Doing this retrains past patterns of behavior so they align more closely with the patterns of your exemplars.

One way of creating space for reason in your thinking is to ask yourself what your exemplars would do if they were in your position. It's the natural next step. Once you imagine them watching, you make decisions and put them into action. If, for instance, you're making an investment decision, ask yourself, "What would Warren Buffett do?" Likewise, ask yourself, "How would I pitch this idea to my personal board of directors? What kinds of factors would they care about? What kinds of factors would they dismiss as irrelevant?"

If you imagine your exemplars watching you, you'd tend to do all the things you know they'd want you to do and avoid the things you know would get in the way.

It's important to engage in this thoughtful exercise often. You have to keep doing it until you acquire a new pattern of thinking, feeling, and acting. Keep practicing until the pattern becomes second nature: an element of who you are, rather than just who you want to be.

One strategy for building strength is to practice in a sandbox. As you may have guessed, the sandbox is metaphorical—a situation in which any mistakes you make are relatively inconsequential and easily reversed. A sandbox allows you to make and learn from mistakes while containing their cost. Practicing in a sandbox increases the likelihood that you'll be successful when the stakes are higher and the outcomes more consequential and less reversible.

One reason why you usually start out managing just one other person or a small team, rather than an entire organization, is that your failures are contained. Starting with a small-scale management role is one example of a sandbox. When you're running a whole organization, mistakes are costlier and harder to contain than when you're managing a team.

There's no substitute for practicing with the real thing, yet sandboxes can remove the downside of the mistakes you inevitably make when practicing. At the intelligence agency, we'd always practice and rehearse before an operation in an environment in which it was safe to fail. We treated the practice as if it were the operation itself; we'd do all the things we planned on doing during the operation, and tried to predict and respond to all the things that could conceivably happen. If something didn't go as planned, we would adapt. And sometimes we'd fail. Failing in that sandbox, though, provided a learning opportunity with few real-world consequences, whereas failing in a real operation could cost people their lives.

PART 3

MANAGING WEAKNESS

*Life gets easier when you don't
blame other people and focus on
what you can control.*

—JAMES CLEAR

PART OF TAKING command of your life is controlling
the things you can. Another part is managing the things
you can't—your vulnerabilities or weaknesses.

Think again of the computer analogy we discussed
earlier. You have the power to change your programming, at least to some extent. In some cases, you can
rewrite your existing algorithms, reprogramming how you
respond to, say, emotion or social pressure or threats to
your ego. Rewriting those algorithms is a great way to
build strength.

But sometimes there are harmful algorithms you can't rewrite. You can't change your biological instincts, the inborn tendencies that resist any attempt to change them. Just because you can't change them, however, doesn't mean you can't manage them. Doing so is merely a matter of programming new subroutines into your life that help mitigate or contain the harmful effects. Adding those subroutines is a way of managing weakness.

•

Knowing Your Weaknesses

WE ALL HAVE WEAKNESSES, MANY OF WHICH ARE BUILT into our biology. We are, for instance, vulnerable to being hungry, thirsty, fatigued, sleep deprived, emotional, distracted, or stressed. All of these conditions can push us toward reacting instead of thinking clearly, and blind us to the deciding moments of our lives.

Each of us also has a limited perspective on things: we can see and know only so much. In addition, we have inbuilt tendencies to form judgments and opinions even in the absence of knowledge. We've seen that our instincts for self-preservation, group membership, hierarchy, and territoriality can all trigger bad judgments that harm us and the people around us.

Some of our weaknesses aren't built into our biology; instead they are acquired through habit, and stay with us by force of inertia.

Bad habits are easy to acquire when there is a delay between action and consequence. If you eat a chocolate bar or skip a workout today, you're not going to suddenly go from healthy to unhealthy. Work late and miss dinner with your family a couple nights, and it won't damage your relationship. If you spend today on social media instead of doing work, you're not going to get fired. However, these choices can end up becoming habits through repetition and accumulate into disaster.

The formula for failure is a few small errors consistently repeated. Just because the results aren't immediately felt doesn't mean consequences aren't coming. You are smart enough to know the potential results; you just don't necessarily realize when they're coming. While good choices repeated make time your friend, bad ones make it your enemy.*

Examples of Inbuilt Weaknesses	Examples of Acquired Weaknesses
Hunger	Acting on emotional impulse
Thirst	Doing less than you're capable of
Fatigue	Refusing to start something because of fear
Sleep deprivation	
Emotion	Seeing only your own point of view
Distraction	Coasting on your talent without hard work
Stress	
Limitations in perspective	
Cognitive biases	

Whatever our weaknesses and whatever their origins, the defaults will handily take command of our lives if we don't manage them. Moreover, we're often unaware when they do.

---

* Jim Rohn said, "One definition of failure is making a few errors in judgment repeated every day." And a summary of James Clear's excellent book *Atomic Habits* is that good habits make time your friend and bad ones make it your enemy.

The Two Ways of Managing Weakness

There are two ways to manage your weaknesses. The first is to build your strengths, which will help you overcome the weaknesses you've acquired. The second is to implement safeguards, which will help you manage any weaknesses you're having trouble overcoming with strength alone. In addition, safeguards help us manage weaknesses that are impossible to overcome—for example, the ones we owe to our biological limitations.

How to Manage Inbuilt Weaknesses	How to Manage Acquired Weaknesses
Safeguards	Strength + safeguards

We saw in Part 2 how strength can overcome weaknesses that we've acquired. For example, developing self-control empowers you to overcome emotion-driven behavior and avoid the regrets it produces. Developing self-confidence empowers you to overcome inertia and execute difficult decisions. It empowers you to overcome social pressure so that you have the strength to go against the crowd. It also empowers you to overcome your ego, acknowledge your deficiencies, and start on the path to doing and being better.

Blind Spots

Some of our weaknesses are the limitations on what we can know, our *blind spots*. We're all familiar with perceptual blind spots—our inability to see accurately beyond a certain distance, and in environments without enough light. We have deaf spots, too; we can't hear sounds below a certain volume or above a certain pitch.

What's true of perception is also true of cognition—our ability to think and judge. The cognitive capacities we've inherited from natural selection weren't designed to achieve maximum accuracy, but only enough to increase our chances of survival and reproduction. In fact, some of these capacities weren't designed for accuracy at all. They exist to prompt us to avoid serious threats to our survival and reproductive potential.

Think of how a rabbit bolts even if you don't pose a real threat to it. Rabbits have this behavioral tendency because, from an evolutionary perspective, they know it's better to be safe than sorry. The survival cost of a false negative is much higher than the cost of a false positive. Many of our cognitive biases work the same way. They were originally designed to bias us toward behaviors that promoted survival and reproduction, and away from behaviors that might compromise them.

For example, both falling in with a group and acting swiftly on the basis of limited information had survival value for our prehistoric ancestors. But both tendencies can trigger errors in judgment, and provide us with additional blind spots.

Knowing about Your Blind Spots Isn't Enough

It's not enough to know about your biases and other blind spots. You have to take steps to manage them. If you don't, the defaults will take control.

Some blind spots are due to our perspective. None of us can know everything about a situation from every angle. Think of poker players. If a player had complete information about who had which cards, they wouldn't make any mistakes. As it is, players can see only their own cards and just the ones dealt faceup. Because they are blind to the other hands, they make mistakes.

While we can only guess why other people do what they do in poker or any other situation, our biggest blind spot tends to be knowing our own weaknesses. There's a famous quote from Richard Feynman: "The first principle is that you must not fool yourself—and you are the easiest person to fool."[1]

We fail to see our own weaknesses for three main reasons.

First, those flaws can be hard for us to detect because they're part of the way we're accustomed to thinking, feeling, and acting. Flawed behavior has become ingrained through a long process of habit formation. Those flaws are part of who we are, even if it's not in line with who we want to be.

Second, seeing our flaws bruises our egos—especially when those flaws are behaviors that are deeply ingrained. They're different from shortcomings like, say, lacking a technical skill, because they feel like a referendum on the kind of person we think we are. We are territorial about how we see ourselves and tend to dismiss information that challenges our self-image.

Third, we have a limited perspective. It is very hard to understand a system that we are a part of. Just as you look back on your sixteen-year-old self and wonder what you were thinking, your future self will look back on your current self and think the same thing. Your present self is blind to the perspective of your future self.

Perspective and human nature make it hard to see our own flaws, and yet it's easy to see the flaws in others. We are practically experts about where our colleagues and friends are weak and where they are strong. It's hard to accept, however, that others might see us just as clearly in kind. When we get feedback about our own weaknesses from the world, it's a rare opportunity for getting better and getting closer to the kind of people we really want to be. Use these opportunities wisely!

Blind Spots on the USS *Benfold*

The story of the USS *Benfold* provides an important example of how to recognize and overcome blind spots.[2]

The *Benfold* was one of the worst-performing warships in the entire US Navy. Commissioned in 1996 for duty in the Pacific Fleet, it housed one of the Navy's most advanced arsenals of missiles and technology at the time. Its radar system was so advanced that it could track a bird from fifty miles. Its mission was to be prepared for war at all times. But it was falling short.

Despite otherwise brilliant military careers, previous commanders had been unable to turn its performance around. So much of a ship's performance comes down to people, not technology.

There's nothing more important for a leader than getting the most out of your crew. Often that comes down to removing obstacles that limit potential. All the technology in the world isn't going to make you better if the people using it are checked out.

The destiny of the USS *Benfold* changed the day Michael Abrashoff was named commander. He was in his mid-thirties when the Navy offered him the *Benfold*, his first sea command. At the time, he said, the "dysfunctional ship had a sullen crew that resented being there and could not wait to get out of the Navy." And yet, in under twenty months, Abrashoff turned the *Benfold* into one of the highest-performing ships in the Navy. And he did it within a stifling hierarchy.

But how?

What's incredible is how he *didn't* do it. He didn't fire or demote anyone. He didn't change the hierarchy. He didn't change any technology. The only real change was within himself. He started to identify his potential blind spots, and to look at the world from the crew's perspective.

Abrashoff observed one of the ship's usual Sunday afternoon cookouts shortly after assuming command, and noticed a long line of sailors waiting to get their lunch while officers cut to the head of the line to get their food. Not only that, but after getting their food, the officers went to a private deck to eat apart from the sailors. Imagine you're a sailor on the ship and your boss comes and hops the line in front of you. What message does this send? Does it make you want to go all in on your job? Does it make you want to come up with new ideas to help the ship?

"The officers weren't bad people," Abrashoff recalls, "they just didn't know any different. It's always been that way." Rather than approaching the officers and telling them what to do (a typical command-and-control approach that rarely works in the long term), Abrashoff simply went to the end of the line.

A supply officer approached him and said, "You don't understand. You go to the head of the line." Abrashoff shrugged this off, saying it didn't seem right to him. He waited in line, got his food, and then sat down with the sailors. The next weekend everyone waited in line and ate together. No command was ever issued.

From the start, Abrashoff knew you can't simply order people to be better. Even if that appears to work, the results are short term and the consequences enormous. It doesn't matter if you're on a ship or running a manufacturing company. You don't tap into people's resourcefulness, intelligence, and skills by command-and-control.

"Show me an organization in which employees take ownership, and I will show you one that beats its competitors," says Abrashoff. "Captains need to see the ship from the crew's perspective. They need to make it easy and rewarding for crew members to express themselves and their ideas."[3]

There is a gap in our thinking that comes from believing that the way we see the world is the way the world really works. It's only when we change our perspective—when we look at the situation through the eyes of other people—that we realize what we're missing. We begin to appreciate our own blind spots and see what we've been missing.

Protecting Yourself with Safeguards

THERE ARE MANY INBUILT BIOLOGICAL VULNERABILITIES that can impede good judgment: sleep deprivation, hunger, fatigue, emotion, distraction, stress from feeling rushed, and being in an unfamiliar environment are just some examples. We can't avoid finding ourselves in these conditions from time to time. But we can implement safeguards to protect us from our defaults when we are.

Safeguards are tools for protecting ourselves from ourselves—from weaknesses that we don't have the strength to overcome.

Here's a simple example. Suppose you want to start eating a healthier diet. You make this task exponentially harder on yourself if you inhabit an unhealthy environment—if, say, your pantry and fridge are full of junk food. Purging your home of all junk food is a safeguard. It protects you against impulsively ripping open a bag of potato chips when you're feeling hungry or bored. Of course, you can still go to the store and buy chips, but that's a lot of work. You have to think, plan, and act. In the time it takes you to do all that, you might think better of your options, and choose to eat something more in line with your health goals.

Purging your home of all junk food is an example of one safeguarding strategy: increasing the amount of "friction" required to do something that's contrary to your long-term goals. There are lots of safeguard strategies, though. My favorites include prevention, creating rules for yourself, making checklists, shifting your frame of reference, and making the invisible visible. Let's talk about each strategy.

Safeguard Strategy 1: Prevention

The first kind of safeguard aims at preventing problems before they happen. One way to do this is to avoid decision-making in unfavorable conditions. Stress, for instance, is a big contributor to bad decisions. Some studies have shown that stress short-circuits the deliberation process—it undermines the systematic evaluation of alternatives that's needed for effective decision-making.[1]

Alcoholics Anonymous has a helpful safeguard for its members. They call it HALT—an acronym that stands for Hungry, Angry, Lonely, and Tired. When you feel like having a drink, they say, ask yourself whether any of these conditions apply. If so, deal with the real problem—hunger, anger, loneliness, or fatigue—instead of reaching for a drink.

You can use the principles behind HALT as a safeguard for decision-making in general. If you have an important decision to make, ask yourself: "Am I hungry? Am I angry or otherwise emotional? Am I lonely or otherwise stressed by my circumstances, such as being in an unfamiliar environment or pressed for time? Am I tired, sleep-deprived, or physically fatigued?" If the answer is yes to any of these questions, avoid making the decision if you can. Wait for a more opportune time. Otherwise, your defaults will take over.

Safeguard Strategy 2: Automatic Rules for Success

Reactive choices are automatic responses to a stimulus. Most of these responses are below the level of consciousness: We're not even aware of them. Sometimes we're able to slow down enough to override our ingrained responses, but this requires a lot of conscious effort on our part. Fortunately, there's an easier way: creating new behaviors that help you get what you want. Think of them as automatic rules for success.

Nothing forces you to accept the ingrained behaviors and rules from your upbringing and life circumstances. You can decide to eliminate them at any time, and replace them with better ones.

In my conversation with Nobel laureate Daniel Kahneman, the godfather of cognitive biases and thinking errors, he revealed an unexpected way we can improve our judgment: replacing decisions with rules.[2] It turns out that rules can help us automate our behavior to put us in a position to achieve success and accomplish our goals.

When we make decisions, we often think of the goals we want to achieve and work backward to identify the means of achieving them. If you want to get in shape, you start going to the gym and eating healthier. If you want to save more money, you might hide part of your paycheck from yourself every week. We use our willpower to accomplish these goals. Once they're accomplished, we often go back to the default behavior we had before. Eventually we realize we're back where we don't want to be, so we begin the entire process again.

This approach is flawed. It involves constant decision-making and effort. Choosing goals is necessary but not sufficient for accomplishing them. You also need to pursue those goals consistently. That means continuing every day to make choices in pursuit of your goals. Every day, you have to choose to work out or to skip dessert. As these choices add up, it becomes harder, not easier, to consistently make choices that move you toward your goals and not away from them.

Making all these choices requires a lot of sustained effort. When we cave into something we didn't want to do, we offer ourselves convenient excuses: "I had a long day," or "I forgot my gym clothes," or "I have a lot of prep for tomorrow's meeting." Eventually it becomes easier to make those excuses than to make the choices that lead us to our goals.

When it comes to your health, just like many other elements of your life, environment determines behavior. Your environment makes one path easier than another.* It's easier to make healthy food choices if the only foods available to you are good for you. It's also easier to stick to a consistent pattern of choices if you're in your familiar operating environment. When you're in an unfamiliar environment, it's harder to maintain your familiar patterns of behavior, which is why a lot of people stop exercising or eating healthy when they travel.

Your environment isn't just your physical surroundings. It also includes people. Sometimes it's hard saying no to someone. We're wired in a way that makes us want to be liked by others, and we're afraid that saying no to someone will make

---

*An idea from *The Path of Least Resistance* by Robert Fritz. Robert talks about how structure determines behavior.

them like us less. Saying no to someone repeatedly can be even more difficult. We might say no when our friend offers us a sugary beverage after a workout one day, but if he does it three days in a row, we cave. That's only human.

We're also wired to want to fit in with other people. Think of how often you have ended up having a social drink when you really just wanted water. Your friends or colleagues ordered first—a glass of wine, say—and you somehow felt guilty about not ordering a drink yourself. So, you order wine too and compromise on what you really want.

Why not bypass individual choices altogether and create an automatic behavior—a rule—that requires no decision-making in the moment and that gets no pushback from others? Why not set a rule that you order a social drink only when you actually feel like one, and never just to fit in with what the group is doing?

Similarly, suppose your goal is to drink less soda.* Rather than deciding on a case-by-case basis whether you're going to drink soda—something that requires a lot of effort and that is prone to error—make a rule instead. For example, "I only drink soda at dinner on Friday," or maybe, "I don't drink soda at all." Having a rule means not having to decide at every meal. The execution path is short, and less error prone.

In a quirk of psychology, people typically don't argue with your personal rules. They just accept them as features of who you are. People question decisions, but they respect rules.

Kahneman told me his favorite rule was never to say yes to a request on the phone. He knows that he wants people to like him, so he wants to say yes in the moment, but after filling up his schedule with things that didn't make him happy, he de-

---

* Like my friend Annie Duke, who gave me this example.

cided to be more vigilant about what he agrees to do and why. When people ask him for things over the phone now, he says something along the lines of, "I'll have to get back to you after I think about it." Not only does this give him time to think without the immediate social pressure, but it also allows a lot of these requests to just drop away because people choose not to follow up. He rarely gets back to any of these people and says yes.*

After speaking with Kahneman, I spent some time thinking about what automatic rules I could create for myself so that my desire in the moment didn't overpower my ultimate desire.

The way I did this was to imagine a film crew following me around documenting how successful I was.† Regardless of whether I was a success or not, how would I act to show someone I deserved my success? What would I want them to see? What am I doing that I would want them not to see because I'm embarrassed or ashamed?

When I run this experiment by people, I am constantly surprised. We all know something we could do to improve our odds of success. And we all know something we can stop doing that would also improve our odds of success.

Just because I can't control all the things I need to do doesn't mean I can't control when I do them. The version of me that I'd want the film crew to see focused on what mattered.

Using this prompt, I decided to create space every day to work on the biggest opportunities. I imagined the film crew

---

*Another effective rule I've seen is that if you wouldn't move something out of your schedule in the next two days for it, just say no.

†I know I did not come up with this thought experiment but I'm unsure whom to give credit to.

watching me make breakfast for the kids and then going to work. While the crew would be expecting to see meetings and people asking me for things, what they'd see is no calls or meetings until lunch so I could spend time working on the most important opportunity. This is where my no-meetings-before-lunch rule came from.*

We're taught our whole lives to follow rules, and yet no one ever told us about how we can create powerful rules that help us get what we want. I find it hard to go to the gym three days a week, so my rule is I go every day. I do not feel like going to the gym every day. In fact, some days I hate it. I also know it's easier to follow my rule than to break it. When it comes to the gym, going every day is easier than going some days.

Creating personal rules is a powerful technique for protecting yourself from your own weaknesses and limitations. Sometimes those rules have surprising benefits.

Safeguard Strategy 3: Creating Friction

Another safeguarding strategy is to increase the amount of effort it takes to do things that are contrary to your goals. I used to find myself checking my email whenever I have a second. I'd check it before I got out of bed, on the walk home from work, in line at the grocery store.

It's easy to tell myself that I'm not the only one, that everyone does this too. The dopamine hit of something new prevents many of us from working on our priorities. It isn't just that I was spending too much time on email, though, it's that

---

* I'd love to hear your automatic rules. Email shane@fs.blog with the subject "Automatic Rule" and let me know.

email could hijack my time from what's important. The scary thing is, I often *wanted* it to take me away from what I was supposed to be doing.

Consider a major report I needed to complete early in my career. I would get to work and rather than write the report, which was clearly the most important thing for me to do, I'd check my email. If there was anything in my inbox that required even a modicum of attention, I'd tell myself I needed to do that before starting on the report. And, of course, by the time I was done with that first email, more had come in that needed attention. It didn't take much to convince myself I needed to do that before I started. Only near the end of the workday would I finally sit down to write the report, mentally exhausted.

When you step back and think about it for a second, I was giving one of the most important things I wanted to do the worst of myself. Email, which I dread on the best of days, was getting my most energetic and creative self. Many of us do this with our partners too. By the time everything we need to do over the course of a long day is finished, we're exhausted. And this is the time we give to our spouse, the most important person in our lives!

If there were a recipe for accumulated disaster, it would be giving the best of ourselves to the least important things and the worst of ourselves to the most important things.

The path to breaking bad habits is making your desired behavior the default behavior. To get on track with the report, I told my colleagues that until the report was submitted, I'd buy them all lunch if they caught me with my email open before 11:00 a.m. My being competitive and not wanting to buy them lunch created enough friction to keep me from checking it first thing in the morning.

I'd work free from distraction all morning. In the afternoon, I'd do email, take calls, and attend or conduct meetings. It's incredible how much I got done.

It's easy to underestimate the role ease plays in decision-making. Since behavior follows the path of least resistance, a surprisingly successful approach is to add friction where you find yourself doing things you don't want to do.

Safeguard Strategy 4: Putting in Guardrails

Another safeguarding strategy is to formulate operating procedures for yourself because you know from hard experience when your defaults tend to override your decision-making. The defaults prevent us from seeing what's actually happening and from responding in ways aligned with our best self-image.

We've already discussed setting automatic rules such as Kahneman's resolution to not say yes to things on the phone, and avoiding making important decisions under unfavorable conditions. There are other effective safeguarding procedures, though, that also force you to slow down in the moment, creating a pocket of time in which to think more clearly about any situation. These procedures make us take a step back and ask, "What am I trying to achieve?" and "Is this moving me closer to that or further away?" These seem like basic questions, but they're often forgotten in the heat of the moment.

Checklists, for instance, offer a simple way to override your defaults. Pilots go through a preflight checklist every time they fly. Surgeons go through preoperative checklists every time they operate. You might have a packing checklist every time you travel. In each of these cases, the checklist acts as a safeguard, forcing us to slow down whatever we're doing and go back to basics: "What am I trying to accomplish? And what are the things I need to accomplish it?" Questions like these are the guardrails that will keep you on the road to success.*

Safeguard Strategy 5: Shifting Your Perspective

Each of us sees things only from a particular point of view. Nobody can possibly see everything. That doesn't mean, however, that we can't shift the way we see things in any given situation.

In physics, a frame of reference is a set of coordinates for observing events. Different observers occupy different frames of reference, and what's visible from one isn't necessarily visible from another. For example, you occupy one frame of reference if you're seated in a traveling train car, while I occupy a different one if I'm standing at the station, watching your train pass by. Within your frame of reference, you and the bench on which you're sitting are stationary. From mine, though, you and the bench are both moving fast.

Imagine now that it were possible for you to shift your frame of reference. What if, for instance, I were live streaming the approach of your train to you? You would then be able to see yourself and your position from my perspective, giving you more information about your situation that wasn't visible from your frame of reference. Suppose your train were on a collision course with an obstacle on the tracks ahead that was only visible from my frame of reference. Within your view, everything would seem fine. You wouldn't know you were headed toward disaster. Shifting your frame of reference and seeing things from

---

* Two effective questions I ask my kids to slow them down and have them think: (1) Do you want to put water or gasoline on this situation? And (2), Is this behavior going to get you what you want?

my perspective would give you crucial information and enable you to take steps to avoid a catastrophe.

What applies in the train example applies to many other cases. While you might be seated on your couch reading this book and not moving at all, from the sun's point of view, you're moving at sixty-seven thousand miles per hour around it. Having an outside perspective on your situation allows you to see more of what's actually happening. Changing your perspective changes what you see.

Shifting your frame of reference is a powerful safeguard against blind spots. Earlier, we saw that Michael Abrashoff was able to turn around the performance of the USS *Benfold* by shifting his frame of reference. Rather than continuing to see things from the *Benfold*'s established frame of reference—a frame in which it was normal for officers to treat sailors as second-class citizens—Abrashoff shifted his frame of reference and looked at things instead from the perspective of ordinary sailors and ordinary fairness.

I once had a coworker who was also a friend. One day he walked into my office with some news. "I figured out what I'm doing wrong," he said. "I'm so busy trying to prove to everyone I'm right that I can't see the world from their point of view."

The problem wasn't that he wasn't smart. He was. It wasn't that he didn't work hard. He did. The problem was that he couldn't relate to other people because he hadn't even made any effort to see things through their eyes. Now he'd come to realize it himself and started to change his behavior.

From that point on, whenever he discussed something with anyone at work, he would start by offering his impressions of how the other person saw things. Then he would ask, "What did I miss?"

Asking this question is a clever move. It implies that he's open to correction and gives the other person a chance to correct him. One of the deepest-rooted human instincts is to correct other people, so by asking this question, he makes it easy for the other person to engage with him. Then, if the other person does in fact correct him, it reveals to him which factors are most important to that person.

When the other person is done answering that first question, my friend still doesn't offer his own thoughts right away. He first asks a follow-up: "What else did I miss?"

This approach to interpersonal communication is an example of a reference-shifting safeguard. Asking the two questions, and listening to the answers people give him, forces him to see things through other people's eyes. Taking the time to do that protects him against a tendency that he identified as a weakness.

A few months after making the change, he became a conduit between his team and the rest of the organization. As time went on, people started asking that he accompany his boss to meetings. When his boss eventually moved to a new role, everyone wanted him to fill the vacancy. He never even had to ask.

How to Handle Mistakes

MISTAKES ARE AN UNAVOIDABLE PART OF LIFE. EVEN THE most skilled people make mistakes, because there are so many factors beyond our knowledge and control that impact our success. This is true especially when we're pushing the boundaries of knowledge or potential. On the frontier of what we can know or do, there are no wagon tracks to follow, no familiar landmarks, no mile markers, no road maps to guide us. We're moving forward without the benefit of anyone else's hindsight. Missteps will happen. Part of taking command of our lives is managing those missteps when they do happen.

When things don't work out the way we'd like, most of us default to blaming the world rather than ourselves. This is a form of what psychologists call *self-serving bias*: a tendency to evaluate things in ways that protect or enhance our self-image, which I mentioned earlier when discussing self-accountability. When people succeed at something, they tend to attribute their success to their own ability or effort: "I'm really smart"; "I worked really hard"; "I knew all the angles." By contrast, when people fail at something, they tend to attribute their failure to external factors: "My boss doesn't like me," "The test was unfair," etc.

In other words, "Heads, I'm right. Tails, I'm not wrong."

If you got some results you didn't want, the world is telling you at least one of two things:

(a) you were unlucky;
(b) your ideas about how things work were wrong.

If you were unlucky, trying again with the same approach should lead to a different outcome. When you repeatedly don't get the outcomes you want, though, the world is telling you to update your understanding.

Many people don't want to hear that their ideas are wrong. They don't want to be conscious of the flaws in their thinking and would prefer instead to sleepwalk through life. They do this in part because recognizing that their ideas are wrong is a blow to their self-image: it's proof that they're not as smart or knowledgeable as they've believed themselves to be. That's the ego default at work.

If you want to see whether your thinking is wrong, you need to make it visible. Making what was previously invisible visible gives us the best chance of seeing what we knew and what we thought at the time we made a decision. Relying on memory won't work because the ego distorts information to make us look better than we actually were.

Once you realize that it's time to update your ideas, though, changing what you believe about the world requires a lot of work. So people tend to ignore what the world is trying to tell them. They keep doing what they've always done and keep getting the same results. That's the inertia default at work.

Mistakes Present Us with a Choice

As with anything else, there are better and worse ways of handling mistakes. The world doesn't stop just because you made a mistake. Life goes on, and you need to go on too. You can't simply throw your hands up and walk away. There are other decisions to make, other things to accomplish, and hopefully you won't repeat that kind of mistake in the future.

Everyone makes mistakes because everyone has limitations. Even you. Trying to avoid responsibility for your decisions, your actions, or their outcomes, though, is tantamount to pretending you don't have limitations. One thing that sets exceptional people apart from the crowd is how they handle mistakes and whether they learn from them and do better as a result.

Mistakes present a choice: whether to update your ideas, or ignore the failures they've produced and keep believing what you've always believed. More than a few of us choose the latter.

The biggest mistake people make typically isn't their initial mistake. It's the mistake of trying to cover up and avoid responsibility for it. The first mistake is expensive; the second one costs a fortune.

My kids learned this the hard way. One day, I came home to find a weird piece of broken glass on the floor. I held it up and asked what had happened, and they pleaded ignorance. When I opened the garbage, though, and moved a sheet of paper that seemed to have been carefully placed on top, I found the remains of a shattered vase. I gave my kids one final opportunity to change their story. With all the confidence preteens could muster, they stuck to it. When the consequences came, it wasn't for breaking the vase, it was for lying.

There are three problems with covering up mistakes. The

first is that you can't learn if you ignore your mistakes. The second is that hiding them becomes a habit. The third is that the cover-up makes a bad situation worse.

Admitting error and correcting course is a time-saver that empowers you to avoid making more mistakes in the future. However, mistakes also provide rare opportunities for getting closer to the kind of person you want to be, should you choose to heed their lessons. Use those opportunities wisely! Don't squander them.

The four steps to handling mistakes more effectively are as follows: (1) accept responsibility, (2) learn from the mistake, (3) commit to doing better, and (4) repair the damage as best you can.

Step 1: Accept Responsibility

If you've taken command of your life, you need to acknowledge any contribution you've made to a mistake and take responsibility for what happens afterward. Even if the mistake isn't entirely your fault, it's still your problem, and you still have a role to play in handling it.

When mistakes happen, the emotion default works hard to usurp control over the situation. It will take over if you let it. This is the opposite of taking command, leaving your life's direction up to an emotional whim. It's essential to keep your emotions in check. If you haven't worked on building that strength, then there's not much you can do. That's why it's important to practice continually.

Step 2: Learn from the Mistake

Take time to reflect on what you contributed to the mistake, by exploring the various thoughts, feelings, and actions that got you here. If it's an emergency, and you don't have time to reflect at the moment, be sure to come back to it. If you don't identify the problem's causes, after all, you can't fix them. And if you can't fix them, you can't do better in the future. Instead, you'll be doomed to repeat the same mistake over and over.

If you reach this stage and you find yourself blaming other people or saying things like, "This isn't fair!" or "Why did this happen to me?" then you haven't accepted responsibility for the mistake. You need to go back to Step 1.

Step 3: Commit to Doing Better

Formulate a plan for doing better in the future. It could be a matter of building a strength like greater self-accountability or greater self-confidence. Or it could be a matter of installing a safeguard like my friend and coworker did when he realized he'd been failing to see things from other people's points of view. Either way, you need to make a plan for doing better in the future, and follow through on that plan. Only then will you be able to change how you do things, and avoid repeating the mistakes of the past.

Step 4: Repair the Damage as Best You Can

Most times it's possible to repair the damage caused by a mistake. The longer your relationship with a person and the more consistent your behavior has been, the easier it is to repair. That doesn't mean it happens instantly, though. Just as it takes a while for a wound to heal, it takes a while for a relationship to heal. It's not enough to accept the impact of your behavior and sincerely apologize. You need to be consistent in doing better going forward. Any immediate deviation quickly reverses any repair.

Not all mistakes are like this. Some mistakes have consequences that are irreversible. The key here is not letting a bad situation become a worse situation.

A friend of mine is the general manager of a major sports team. When talking about mistakes, he told me about a mentor of his who had made a "bad trade" based on impulse, not reason. After the paperwork was signed, he couldn't take it back. His mentor knew it was a mistake before the player suited up for their first game. His inner voice, the inner saboteur we all have, told him he was an imposter and now the whole world knew it. It told him he was an idiot. That little voice undid years of exceptional player management, eroding his confidence and paralyzing him, rendering him unable to make effective decisions under uncertainty. He kept thinking that gathering more data would help him remove uncertainty. It wasn't long before he lost his job.

Mistakes turn into anchors if you don't accept them. Part of accepting them is learning from them and then letting them go. We can't change the past, but we can work to undo the effects it's had on the future.

The most powerful story in the world is the one you tell yourself. That inner voice has the power to move you forward or anchor you to the past. Choose wisely.

PART 4

DECISIONS: CLEAR THINKING IN ACTION

If you choose not to decide, you still have made a choice.

—NEIL PEART

ONCE YOU HAVE reprogrammed your defaults to create space for clear thinking, you must master the skill of decision-making.

Decisions are different from choices. If you casually select an option from a range of alternatives, you've made a choice. If you react without thinking, you've made an unconscious choice. But neither of these is the same as a decision. A decision is a choice that involves conscious thought.

The decision = the judgment that a
certain option is the best one

Often what seems like poor judgment in hindsight doesn't even register as a decision in the moment. When the defaults conspire, we react without thinking. And that reaction doesn't even count as a decision. Once we register the opportunity to make a conscious choice, the question becomes: How can we make the best decision possible?

The decision itself should represent the outcome of the decision-making process. That process is about weighing your options with the aim of selecting the best one, and it's composed of four stages: defining the problem, exploring possible solutions, evaluating the options, and finally making the judgment and executing the best option. We will discuss each of these components in detail throughout this chapter.

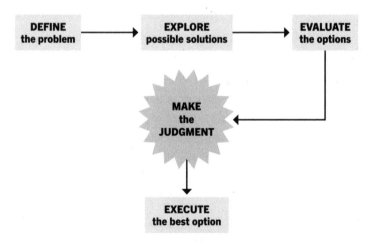

The Decision-Making Process

DEFINE
the problem ⟶ **EXPLORE**
possible solutions ⟶ **EVALUATE**
the options

MAKE
the
JUDGMENT

EXECUTE
the best option

The decision = the judgment that a certain option is the best one

If you don't apply this process, your choice doesn't necessarily count as a decision.

Small children tend to make choices without any kind of evaluation. Sometimes adults do too. Perhaps it's because we have to make a choice so quickly that we don't have time to evaluate the options. Or maybe it's because we let habit choose for us, the inertia of past choices carrying us through the present moment without exploring our options. Or maybe it's just that we let our emotions make choices without even realizing it—momentary anger, fear, or desire preempting evaluation and pushing us to act without thinking or reason.

None of these examples count as decisions. That doesn't mean we're not responsible for them. We are! It simply means we're not reasoning. We're not consciously thinking. Instead, we're reacting, and giving up our deciding moment to our defaults. It's in these moments that we often do something contrary to what we'd decide is best if we reasoned instead of reacted. When we react without reason, we cause more problems than we solve. If only we had the hindsight of our future selves as our foresight now!

Not every bad decision is rushed, nor is every good one made slowly. It's not that simple.

People mistake choosing for decisiveness and the decision-making process for waffling. Part of what makes slowing down and reasoning through a problem difficult is that, to the outside observer, it might look like inaction. But inaction is a choice.

When the stakes are low, inaction hurts you more than speed. Sometimes it's better just to make a quick choice and not spend time deliberating. Why waste time evaluating if an action is inconsequential and its effects are easily reversed? For example, if there are two identical squat racks in the gym and both are momentarily open, it makes no difference which one you take. If you wait and decide, they'll both be taken by someone else. Just choose either one.

When the stakes are higher, though, speed can hurt you. If an action could have a major impact on your life or your business and its effects can't be reversed, you must decide and not merely choose. In these cases, the magnitude of the potential losses makes careful decision-making a worthwhile investment of your time. In these cases, evaluate the options and decide. Don't just choose.

The next few sections describe some tools for reasoning better when making decisions. They won't solve every decision-making problem, because no tool is right for every job; each has its uses and limitations. You need multiple tools in your toolbox. Otherwise, you end up solving the wrong problems. As the old adage says, "If the only tool you have is a hammer, you tend to see every problem as a nail."

Knowing how to use these tools depends on keeping your defaults in check so you *can* reason. If you can't, you'll just react with one of your defaults. While you might get the outcomes you desire for a while, it's only a matter of time before lack of thinking catches up to you. It's only after you've mastered the defaults that the tools I describe become useful.

If you can't keep those in check—if you're easily

swayed by emotion, if you can't adapt to change, if you value being right more than doing what's best—then all the tools in the world aren't going to help you. The defaults will overwhelm you, rout your decision-making process, and seize control of your life.

•

Define the Problem

THE FIRST PRINCIPLE OF DECISION-MAKING IS THAT THE decider needs to define the problem.* If you're not the one making the decision, you can suggest the problem that needs to be solved, but you don't get to define it. Only the person responsible for the outcome does. The decision-maker can take input from anywhere—bosses, subordinates, colleagues, experts, etc. However, the responsibility to get to the bottom of the problem—to sort fact from opinion and determine what's really happening—rests with them.

Defining the problem starts with identifying two things: (1) what you want to achieve, and (2) what obstacles stand in the way of getting it.

Unfortunately, people too often end up solving the wrong problem.

---

* I learned this firsthand at operational meetings. Only the person in charge of the operation could define the objective, the goals, and the problems. Everyone else could suggest things but one person had to own the decision, and that person was in charge of the operation. It's been reinforced many times by Adam Robinson, Peter Kaufman, and Randall Stutman.

Perhaps you can relate to this scenario, which I've seen thousands of times over the years. A decision-maker assembles a diverse team to solve a critical and time-sensitive problem. There are ten people in the room all giving input about what's happening—each from a different perspective. Within a few minutes someone announces what they think the problem is, the room goes silent for a microsecond . . . and then everyone starts discussing possible solutions.

Often the first plausible description of the situation defines the problem that the team will try to solve.* Once the group comes up with a solution, the decision-maker feels good. That person then allocates resources toward the idea and expects the problem to be solved. But it isn't. Because the first lens into an issue rarely reveals what the real problem is, so the real problem doesn't get solved.

What's happening here?

The social default prompts us to accept the first definition people agree on and move forward. Once someone states a problem, the team shifts into "solution" mode without considering whether the problem has even been correctly defined. This is what happens when you put a bunch of smart, type A people together and tell them to solve a problem. Most of the time, they end up missing the real problem and merely addressing a symptom of it. They react without reasoning.

Many of us have been taught that solving problems is how we add value. In school, teachers give us problems to solve, and at work our bosses do the same. We've been taught our whole lives to solve problems.

But when it comes to defining problems, we have less ex-

---

*I had witnessed this for years before Randall Stutman pointed out to me what was happening.

perience. Things are often uncertain. We seldom have all the information. Sometimes, there are competing ideas about what the problem is, competing proposals to solve it, and then lots of interpersonal friction. So we're much less comfortable defining problems than solving them, and the social default uses that discomfort. It encourages us to react instead of reason, in order to prove we're adding value. Just solve a problem—*any problem*!

The result: organizations and individuals waste a lot of time solving the wrong problems. It's so much easier to treat the symptoms than find the underlying disease, to put out fires rather than prevent them, or to simply punt things into the future. The problem with this approach is that the fires never burn out, they flare up repeatedly. And when you punt something into the future, the future eventually arrives.

We're busier than ever at work, but most of the time what we're busy doing is putting out fires—fires that started with a poor initial decision made years earlier, which should've been prevented in the first place.

And because there are so many fires and so many demands on our time, we tend to focus on just putting out the flames. Yet as any experienced camper knows, putting out flames doesn't put out the fire. Since all our time is spent running around and putting out the flames, we have no time to think about today's problems, which can create the kindling for tomorrow's fires.

The best decision-makers know that the way we define a problem shapes everyone's perspective about it and determines the solutions. The most critical step in any decision-making process is to get the problem right. This part of the process offers invaluable insight. Since you can't solve a problem you don't understand, defining the problem is a chance to take in lots of relevant information. Only by talking to the experts, seeking the opinions of others, hearing their different perspectives, and sorting out what's real from what's not can the decision-maker understand the real problem.

When you really understand a problem, the solution seems obvious. Later, we'll talk about the tells that reveal when people are solving a problem they don't fully understand.

These two principles follow the example of the best decision-makers:

> **THE DEFINITION PRINCIPLE:** Take responsibility for defining the problem. Don't let someone define it for you. Do the work to understand it. Don't use jargon to describe or explain it.

> **THE ROOT CAUSE PRINCIPLE:** Identify the root cause of the problem. Don't be content with simply treating its symptoms.

I once took over a department where the software would regularly freeze. Solving the problem required physically rebooting the server. (The drawback of working in a top secret facility was our lack of connectivity to the outside world.)

Almost every weekend, one of the people on my team would be called into work to fix the problem. Without fail, he'd have the system back up and running quickly. The outage was small, the impact minimal. Problem solved. Or was it?

At the end of the first month, I received the overtime bill to sign. Those weekend visits were costing a small fortune. We were addressing the symptom without solving the problem. Fixing the real problem required a few weeks of work, instead of a few minutes on the weekend. No one wanted to solve the real problem because it was painful. So we just kept putting out flames and letting the fire reignite.

A handy tool for identifying the root cause of a problem is to ask yourself, "What would have to be true for this problem not to exist in the first place?" Here's another example of this tool put to use:

The ASPCA is one of the largest animal-welfare groups in the United States. It estimates that more than 3 million dogs enter shelters each year and are put up for adoption. Roughly 1.4 million of them are successfully adopted, but that leaves more than 1 million unadopted dogs in the US each year.*

There are only so many people willing to adopt a pet, and only so many pets a given family can handle, so the question facing most shelters is, "How can we get more people to adopt?" But answering that question doesn't make any progress toward a long-term solution.

One shelter took a different approach. The founder of Downtown Dog Rescue in Los Angeles, Lori Weise, asked instead, "What would have to be true for there to be fewer dogs to adopt in the first place?"[1] Weise dug into the data and found that 30 percent of dogs entering a shelter were owner surrenders—pets voluntarily given up by their owners. She found that many times caring owners surrendered their pets because they couldn't afford to feed them and thought someone else could better care for the animal. With this insight, a better and more permanent solution became apparent.

Weise started a new program: Whenever a family came in to surrender a pet, the staff asked if they would prefer to keep

---

* At Farnam Street we use this example in our course Decision by Design, where we teach world-class people to make better decisions. (If you want to be added to the waitlist, just email me at shane@fs.blog with the subject line "DBD Waitlist.")

the pet. If the answer was yes, the staff used their network to help resolve the problem—whether it was just a matter of a ten-dollar rabies shot, or long-term access to pet food. Weise and her team found that it was actually cheaper to help a family feed and keep a pet than to house it at the shelter. More important, the program enabled 75 percent of the families who came in intending to surrender pets to keep them permanently instead.

Identifying the root cause of a problem applies in business too. A company might think that its problem is getting too few new sales, so it marshals resources to get new leads. But what if getting new sales isn't the root of the problem? What if there's an issue with, say, the product itself? The root cause of any problem like this is customer satisfaction, and that's not necessarily the same as getting new customers. It could also be keeping existing customers happy. The way you define a problem changes what you see.

Your defaults are always present, and despite your efforts to follow the Definition Principle and the Root Cause Principle, it's still possible to get sidetracked.

How to Safeguard the Problem-Defining Stage

There are two ways to safeguard this stage of the decision process against our defaults: create a firewall and use time to your advantage.

> **SAFEGUARD:** *Build a problem-solution firewall.* Separate the problem-defining phase of the decision-making process from the problem-solving phase.

A mentor of mine once taught me that the best way to avoid finding the perfect solution to the wrong problem at work, when time allows, is to hold two separate meetings: one to define the problem, and one to come up with the solution.

The most precious resources in any organization are time and the brainpower of your best employees. Asking for two separate meetings to come up with a solution to a problem that seemed obvious to everyone is not an easy sell. But it's worth it. I've used this safeguard for many years, and I've seen it used over and over by people who consistently make good decisions. As soon as they start implementing it, they learn that having a single meeting for both tasks only makes them vulnerable to the social default—either their action-oriented teams will likely spend only a moment or two defining the problem and the rest of the meeting trying to solve it, or everyone will start suggesting solutions to their version of the problem. Either way the meeting won't be as useful as it should be.

When you spend time trying to understand the problem, you realize that you have a room full of people who have insight that you don't have. One way to keep meetings short and avoid the signaling that comes from repeating information that everyone knows is simply asking everyone, "What do you know about this problem that other people in the room don't know?"

That question makes people think. They stop filling the air with ideas everyone already knows and start explaining how they think about the problem.

Not only do you start learning from each other, but you come to understand the problem at a deeper level because you start to see (and hopefully appreciate) different perspectives. Later, when you reconvene at the second meeting, the solutions often become obvious to everyone. And because everyone understands the problem, each person knows how to move their part of the organization in a way that solves it for everyone, not just themselves. An apocryphal quote often attributed to the philosopher Ludwig Wittgenstein sums up this idea: "To understand is to know what to do."*

People go fast in operational environments. If you insert too much process into decisions, you miss the expiring windows of opportunity. But fast-paced environments are a feast for defaults. You need to slow down—but not too much—and use a combination of judgment, principles, and safeguards to make sure you're getting to the best answer possible and thinking clearly. Probing and asking deeper questions slows down the process just enough to dramatically improve your chances of solving the right problem.

Creating space between the definition of a problem and the solution to it works at a personal level too. Give yourself time to get clear on what the problem is before you jump into solving it. More often than not, you'll discover that your first attempt to define the underlying issue is rarely the most accurate.

> **TIP:** Remember that writing out the problem makes the invisible visible. Write down what you think the problem is, and then look at it the next day. If you find yourself using jargon in your description, it's a sign that you don't fully understand the problem. And if you don't understand it, you shouldn't be making a decision about it.

---

*Several people have attributed this quote to Wittgenstein, but a search through the InteLex database of both his published and his unpublished writings reveals it nowhere. Perhaps the closest quotation is from section 199 of his *Philosophical Investigations*: "To understand a sentence means to understand a language. To understand a language means to be master of a technique."

Let's move on to the second way of safeguarding this stage of the decision-making process.

> **SAFEGUARD:** *Use the test of time.* Test whether you're addressing the root cause of a problem, rather than merely treating a symptom, by asking yourself whether it will stand the test of time. Will this solution fix the problem permanently, or will the problem return in the future? If it seems like the latter, then chances are you're only treating a symptom.

Suppose, for example, that Downtown Dog Rescue in Los Angeles had tried to solve its problem with overcrowding by hosting a spring dog-adoption campaign, rather than addressing one of the root causes: pet owners' inability to continue caring for their dogs. The campaign might have succeeded in reducing the number of dogs the rescue housed at the time, but only temporarily. A few months later, the facility would have once again been overcrowded.

Short-term solutions might make sense in the moment, but they never win in the long term. You feel like you're moving forward when you're actually just going in circles. People gravitate toward them because finding a short-term fix signals to others that they're doing something. That's the social default at work. It fools people into mistaking action for progress, the loudest voice for the right one, and confidence for competence. Time eventually reveals short-term solutions to be Band-Aids that cover deeper problems. Don't be fooled!

You can put your energy into short-term solutions or long-term solutions but not both. Any energy that's channeled toward short-term solutions depletes energy that could be put into finding a long-term fix.[2] Sometimes short-term solutions are necessary to create space for long-term solutions. Just make sure you're not putting out flames in the present that will reignite in the future. When the same problem returns again and again, people end up exhausted and discouraged because they never seem to make real progress. Extinguish the fire today so it can't burn you tomorrow.

These principles, safeguards, and tips will keep you from jumping at the social default's whim.

Explore Possible Solutions

ONCE YOU'RE CLEAR ON THE PROBLEM, IT'S TIME TO THINK of possible solutions—ways of overcoming the obstacles to get what you want. The way to come up with possible solutions is by imagining different possible futures—different ways the world could turn out.

One of the most common errors at this stage of the decision-making process is avoiding the brutal realities.

In his book *Good to Great,* author Jim Collins tells the story of his interview with Admiral James Stockdale. During the Vietnam War, Stockdale was the highest-ranking US military officer at the notorious Hỏa Lò prisoner of war camp (sarcastically dubbed the "Hanoi Hilton"). He was tortured over twenty times during an eight-year imprisonment and given no release date, no prisoner rights, and no certainty whether he would survive to see his family again.

When Collins asked Stockdale about his fellow prisoners who didn't survive the camp, the admiral singled out the optimists. "Oh, they were the ones who said, 'We're going to be out by Christmas.' And Christmas would come, and Christmas would go. Then they'd say, 'We're going to be out by Easter.' And Easter would come, and Easter would go. And then Thanksgiving, and then it would be Christmas again. And they died of a broken heart."

After a long pause, he turned to Collins and said, "This is a very important lesson. You must never confuse faith that you will prevail in the end—which you can never afford to lose—with the discipline to confront the most brutal facts of your current reality, whatever they might be."[1]

Collins called this combination of faith in prevailing with the discipline to confront brutal facts the Stockdale Paradox. He says he still carries with him the mental image of Stockdale admonishing the optimists: "We're not getting out by Christmas; deal with it!"

Problems Don't Disappear by Themselves

We all face difficult problems. The defaults narrow our perspective. They narrow our view of the world and tempt us to see things as we wish them to be, not as they are. Only by dealing with reality—the often-brutal truth of how the world really works—can we secure the outcomes we want.

The worst thing we can do with a difficult problem is resort to magical thinking—putting our heads in the sand and hoping the problem will disappear on its own or that a solution will present itself to us.

The future is not like the weather. It doesn't just happen to us. We shape our future with the choices we make in the present, just as our present situation was shaped by choices we made in the past.

Wherever we are now is a reflection of the past choices and

behaviors that got us here. If we're in a happy relationship, we can look back and see the years of effort, communication, negotiation, luck, and (possibly) therapy that got us to this point. If we wake up bleary-eyed and muddleheaded, we can see how excessive drinking the night before disrupted our sleep. If we're operating a successful business, we can see how running lean at the right times, or perhaps doubling down when things weren't so certain, contributed to our current success.

If only we had the benefit of hindsight for the decisions we make today—if only we could see the present with the insight and clarity we have about the past! The philosopher Søren Kierkegaard once said, "Life can only be understood backwards, but it must be lived forwards."

Luckily, there's a way to convert the hindsight of tomorrow into the foresight of today. It's a thought experiment that psychologists call *premortem*. The concept isn't new, it originates in Stoic philosophy. Seneca used *premeditatio malorum* ("the premeditation of evils") to prepare for the inevitable ups and downs of life. The point isn't to worry about problems; it's to fortify and prepare for them.

The hardest setbacks to deal with are the ones we're not prepared for and don't expect. That's why you need to anticipate them before they happen and act now in order to avoid them.

Many people think they're bad problem solvers when in fact they're bad problem anticipators. Most of us don't want to think about more problems; we have enough already. We think that before bad things happen, we'll get a warning, we'll have time to prepare, we'll be ready. But the world doesn't work that way.

Bad things happen to good people all the time. We get laid off without warning. We get into a car accident. Our boss comes into our office and lays into us. A pandemic spreads throughout the world. No warnings. No time to prepare.

Performing a premortem might not save you from every disaster, but you'll be surprised by how many it can save you from. Here's how it works.

What Could Go Wrong?

Imagining what could go wrong doesn't make you pessimistic. It makes you prepared. If you haven't thought about the things that could go wrong, you will be at the mercy of circumstances. Fear, anger, panic—when emotion consumes you, reason leaves you. You just react.

The antidote is this principle:

> **THE BAD OUTCOME PRINCIPLE:** Don't just imagine the ideal future outcome. Imagine the things that could go wrong and how you'll overcome them if they do.

If you've got a presentation to the board next week, imagine all the ways it could go wrong: What if technology fails? What if they can't find the presentation? What if the audience isn't engaged?

Leave nothing out of consideration. Nothing should surprise you. As Seneca said, "We need to envisage every possibility and . . . strengthen the spirit to deal with the things which may conceivably come about."[2]

When bad things happen, there is no two-minute warning where you get a commercial break to prepare. You have to deal with it as it happens. The best decision-makers know that bad things happen, and that they're not immune. They don't just wing it and react. They anticipate and make contingency plans.

And because they're ready, their confidence doesn't crack. The venture capitalist Josh Wolfe likes to say, "Failure comes from a failure to imagine failure."[3]

The bottom line: people who think about what's likely to go wrong and determine the actions they can take are more likely to succeed when things don't go according to plan.

A smart way to assess your options is by using the following principle.

> **THE SECOND-LEVEL THINKING PRINCIPLE:** Ask yourself, "And then what?"

When you solve a problem, you make a change in the world. That change can be either in line with your long-term objectives or not. For example, if you're hungry and you eat a chocolate bar, you've solved the immediate hunger problem, but that solution has consequences: the inevitable sugar crash an hour or two later. If your longer-term goal is to be productive that afternoon, the chocolate bar is not the best solution to your immediate problem.

It's true that eating a chocolate bar once won't ruin your diet or your day. But repeating that seemingly small error in judgment daily over the course of your lifetime will not put you in a position for success. Tiny choices compound. That's why second-level thinking is needed.

Second-Level Thinking

Inside us all, there is a competition between our today self and our future self.* Our future self often wants us to make

---

* This is an idea that came from a conversation with my friend Chris Sparling.

different choices than our today self wants to make. While today you cares about winning the present moment, future you cares about winning the generation. Each of these personalities offers a different perspective on problems. Our future self sees the benefits or consequences of the accumulation of our seemingly insignificant choices.

You can think of first-level thinking as your today self and second-level thinking as your future self.

First-level thinking looks to solve the immediate problem without regard to any future problems a solution might produce. Second-level thinking looks at the problem from beginning to end. It looks past the immediate solution and asks, "And then what?"* The chocolate bar doesn't seem so tempting when you answer this question.

You can't solve a problem optimally unless you consider not just whether it meets your short-term objectives but whether it meets your long-term objectives as well. A failure to think of second-order consequences leads us unknowingly to make bad decisions. You can't ensure the future is easier if you only think about solving the current problem and don't give due consideration to the problems created in the process. This idea is evident when looking back at the US war in Afghanistan.

According to a report issued by the Special Inspector General for Afghanistan Reconstruction,

> Many of the institutions and infrastructure projects the
> United States built were not sustainable. . . . Every mile

---

*The first time I came across this idea was from Garrett Hardin, who asks this very question. For more, see "Three Filters Needed to Think Through Problems," *Farnam Street* (blog), December 14, 2015, https://fs.blog/garrett-hardin-three-filters/.

of road the United States built and every government employee it trained was thought to serve as a springboard for even more improvements and to enable the reconstruction effort to eventually end. However, the U.S. government often failed to ensure its projects were sustainable over the long term. Billions of reconstruction dollars were wasted as projects went unused or fell into disrepair. Demands to make fast progress incentivized U.S. officials to identify and implement short-term projects with little consideration for host government capacity and long-term sustainability.[4]

By contrast, here's an example of the Second-Level Thinking Principle in action. My friend's client—call her Maria—is a mostly self-taught data scientist.* She worked her way up through the startup world and became a reasonably successful executive at a tech company, where she spent five years. Her position recently disappeared overnight, when the company went under.

Her goals are to continue earning an executive's salary (around $180k per year) while working from home and having a schedule that allows her to be present for her family. Ideally, she wants to work for a company committed to social responsibility. She has $100k in the bank, and wants to have a job within two years, but can wait as long as four. She currently has two job offers for less money than she wants, and neither job excites her very much. She's considering going back to school for her master's in the hopes that it'll open up more employment options, but she knows she won't be able to do

---

* This example comes from the course Decision by Design.

schoolwork while holding a full-time position and still have time for her family.

Let's now consider some possible solutions. Maria's options include:

- Going back to school for a master's degree
- Accepting one of the full-time positions she's been offered at $90k per year
- Doing some consulting work
- Continuing to look for other full-time opportunities

Next, consider the immediate outcomes of these options:

- **If Maria goes back to school,** it could mean thirty-plus hours a week doing school-related things. That would mean less time to dedicate to paid work or her family.
- **If she accepts one of the full-time positions she's been offered,** she would be making money and be able to pay her bills. It would be far less than she wants, but she could compensate by tightening her budget and saving more for retirement.
- **If she does consulting work,** there are a lot of unknowns. She doesn't know how much demand there is for her services, or how much she could earn providing them.
- **If she continues looking for full-time opportunities,** she might lose the two job offers she has. She needs to give them a response in a reasonable amount of time.

Now that we have a sense of the immediate outcomes of Maria's options, it's time to apply second-level thinking. We must consider the outcomes of those outcomes, the answer to the question, "And then what?"

Let's apply the Bad Outcome Principle as we go through the options, thinking not just about the case in which everything goes well, but also the case in which things go poorly.

Maria goes back to school:

- **If it goes well:** She gets a scholarship, develops a great network, gains skills, and opens up a lot of opportunities for herself. The new problem in this case is turning those skills into a role that she wants and that pays well.
- **If it goes poorly:** She doesn't learn any skills that people are actually hiring for, and takes on debt in the process. The new problem in this case is paying her bills on top of debt while searching for a job that's even more elusive than before.

We can now see that Maria needs to gather some further information to determine whether going back to school is her best option:

- Whether or not she can get a scholarship
- How well the school is networked in the private sector
- Whether people are hiring for the skills she'll develop and what they're willing to pay
- How long it will take her to make $180k a year with the new skills she'll have

Maria accepts one of the full-time positions she's been offered:

- **If it goes well:** She makes less than she wants, but there's room to grow at the company. There are at least three new problems in this case: (1) figuring out how to close the wage gap and retire when she wants, (2) figuring out how to move up in the company, and (3) finding opportunities outside of work to fulfill her desire for social responsibility.

- **If it goes poorly:** She's in another job she's not passionate about and making less money than she wants. The new problem in this case isn't all that new: she'll be in more or less the same situation she's in right now but with some income.

Here's the further information Maria needs to gather to determine whether accepting one of these full-time positions is her best option:

- Her chances of liking her job
- Her chances of moving up in the company
- What experience the job will give her so she can move on if she wants
- Whether she can go back to school or do consulting work while she does the job

Maria does consulting work:

- **If it goes well:** It could lead to her own business and increased flexibility. The new problem in this case is figuring out how to scale a business.
- **If it goes poorly:** Her consulting opportunities are few and far between, and she misses out on the job offers. The new problem in this case is figuring out her next move. She'll be in the same position she's in now but with less runway: she'll have less time to accept an offer.

We now know what further information Maria needs to gather to evaluate this option:

- Whether people are willing to pay her for her current knowledge and skills
- How much they are willing to pay

Maria's example illustrates an important point about second-level thinking: it not only helps us avoid future problems, it also uncovers information we need to make a better decision—information we didn't know we needed before. It's easy to sit back and think the right information will find you. It won't!

How to Safeguard the Solution-Exploring Stage

Just because you've thought of a couple solutions, though, doesn't mean you've eliminated your blind spots. Binary thinking is when you consider only two options to a problem. When you first look at the choice, it seems simple: We launch the product or we don't. We take the new job or we don't. We get married or we don't. It's black and white: "do" or "do not." There isn't any middle ground.

Most of the time, though, this type of thinking is limiting. Some decisions might seem to come down to a choice between this or that, but there's often another option. The best decision-makers know this, and see binary thinking as a sign that we don't fully understand a problem—that we're trying to reduce the problem's dimensions before fully understanding them.

When we start exploring a problem in detail, things become more complicated before we understand it well enough to see the alternatives.

Problem-solving novices try to reduce a decision to just two options because it creates the false sense that they've gotten to the problem's essence. In reality, they've just stopped thinking. And you never want to stop thinking! Novices fail to see the complexities of a problem that are apparent to a master. Masters see the simplicity hiding in the complexity. As Frederic Maitland purportedly once wrote, "Simplicity is the end result of long, hard work, not the starting point." When we reduce the problem to black-and-white solutions, we need to check to make sure we're the master and not the novice.

This brings us to the next principle of effective problem-solving:

> **THE 3+ PRINCIPLE:** Force yourself to explore at least three possible solutions to a problem. If you find yourself considering only two options, force yourself to find at least one more.

Binary framing is as comfortable as it is passive. Doing the work to add a third option forces us to be creative and really dig into the problem. Even if we don't choose the third option, forcing ourselves to develop it helps us understand the problem better. It gives us more opportunities to align our decisions with our goals, offers more optionality in the future, and increases the chances that we'll be happier with our decision down the road.

There are two safeguards against binary thinking. The first is this:

> **SAFEGUARD:** *Imagine that one of the options is off the table.* Take each of the options you're considering, and one at a time, ask yourself, "What would I do if that were not possible?"

Suppose you're considering what to do about a job where you don't get along with a coworker. Binary thinking tells you to stay or leave. Imagining that one option is off the table forces you to see the problem differently. Imagine that, for some reason, there is absolutely no way to quit your job: You must stay. Now you are forced to see things through a new lens. What could you do to make going to work every day more enjoyable, despite the problem with your coworker? What could you do to remain at your job and still move closer to your goals? What could you do to give yourself more options in the future so you're not stuck feeling powerless? Maybe staying means having a hard conversation with your boss and your coworker that you haven't had yet. Maybe it means putting in for a transfer to another department. Maybe it means asking your boss if you can work remotely.

Now try looking at this situation the other way. Imagine that, for some reason, there is absolutely no way you can stay at your job: You have to leave. What would you do? Would you call up old clients and see if they need help? Would you get hold of people in your network to see if they could make an introduction at their company? Would you pursue every possibility until you found yourself in a better position?

Sometimes we can't do what we want when we want, like leaving a job that's become difficult to endure. But that doesn't mean we're stuck. We can always do something to move forward, putting ourselves in a better position to get more of what we want and less of what we don't. If we can't leave our job, we can at least improve it. If we can't stay, we can prepare to leave. Reframing the problem shows us the next step.

Remember: Limiting ourselves to binary thinking before fully understanding a problem is a dangerous simplification that creates blind spots. False dualities prevent you from seeing alternative paths and other information that might change your mind. On the other hand, taking away one of two clear options forces you to reframe the problem and get unstuck.

Here's the second safeguard against binary thinking:

> **SAFEGUARD:** *Come up with Both-And options.* Try to find ways of combining the binary. Think not in terms of choosing either X or Y, but rather having both X and Y.

Roger Martin, former dean of the Rotman School of Management in Toronto, refers to this technique as *integrative thinking.*[5] Rather than grappling with seemingly opposed binary options, combine them. Simplistic Either-Or options become integrative Both-And options. You can keep costs down *and* invest in a better customer experience. You can stay at your job *and* start a side hustle. You can deliver for your shareholders *and* protect the environment.

F. Scott Fitzgerald once said, "The test of a first-rate intelligence is the ability to hold two opposed ideas in the mind at the same time, and still retain the ability to function. One should, for example, be able to see that things are hopeless and yet be determined to make them otherwise."

Unlike Fitzgerald, though, I don't think you need to have first-rate intelligence to come up with Both-And options. The capacity for combinatorial solutions isn't reserved for the gifted. It's a skill that can be learned and used; it's just a skill that goes untaught. The key is learning to live with the uncomfortable tension between opposing ideas long enough to see that there's a solution that combines the best elements of both. And that's what integrative thinking is all about.

It can be challenging to think this way, yet it's almost always possible. One area where we tend to be pretty good at integrative thinking is vacation planning. We ask everyone involved what they want to do, and then try to find a place that has it all. This is why resorts or cruises offer a long list of activities: the more variety, the more attractive they are to groups with diverse interests. Guests in such places rarely face a hard choice between, say, the beach or the pool. They can have both.

You can apply the same thinking to other areas of your life, including your career. The solution to an unfulfilling job is rarely just one option in the stay-or-go binary, even if it seems that way at first. You can *both* stay *and* begin reaching out to your network. You can *both* apply for jobs *and* go to school in the evenings to acquire a new skill. You can *both* start a creative project *and* do more at your current job to give you the creative outlet you need.

Roger Martin put it this way: "Thinkers who exploit opposing ideas to construct a new solution enjoy a built-in advantage over thinkers who can consider only one model at a time." He's right. Not only do integrative thinkers build an advantage, they also tend to capture exponential upside because they break free of traditional ways of thinking.

Consider Isadore Sharp, who created the luxurious Four Seasons hotel chain. Sharp's first property was a small roadside hotel in the Toronto suburbs. His second was a large convention hotel in the heart of the city. Each property represented one of the conventional operating models of the time: either going small and focusing on personal service or going large and focusing on amenities. The hotel industry was stuck in binary thinking. Rather than choose between them, though, Sharp combined the intimacy of a small hotel with the amenities of a large one. In the process he created a new way of operating and one of the most successful hotel chains of all time.

Our personal lives also benefit from Both-And thinking. For example, we often expect our partners to fulfill 100 percent of our emotional needs. That's a lot to ask of anyone, and many of us experience relationship challenges when disappointments inevitably result. But instead of asking, "Should I stay or leave?" ask instead, "Is there anyone else that could meet some of the emotional needs that my partner can't? Is there a colleague that I could vent to at work? Do I have a friend who shares this interest or who will take this class with me?"

When we think of adding people to our lives, we start to open up Both-And options for ourselves. So instead of the usual relationship binary, "Should I stay or leave?" we start to say, "Whom else can I include in my life to help with everything beyond what my partner does well?"

We don't need a lot of additional options, just a few really good ones. When you hear yourself say, "Either X or Y," it means you're entering the narrow pathway between a rock and a hard place—a binary decision. Digging in and forcing yourself to add credible alternative options allows you to see solutions you may not have considered before.

Opportunity Costs

Thinking better isn't about filling your brain with answers to questions you've seen before. It's not about memorizing what to do and when. It's not about letting other people think for you either. It's about looking beyond the things that are obvious and seeing the things that are hidden from view.

The real world is full of trade-offs, some of which are obvious, and others that are hidden. Opportunity costs are the hidden trade-offs that decision-makers often have trouble assessing. Every decision has at least one of them. Because we can't always do everything we want, picking one thing usually means forgoing another. The ability to size up hidden trade-offs is part of what separates great decision-makers from the rest. It's also a core element of leadership.

Charlie Munger put it this way: "Intelligent people make decisions based on opportunity costs . . . it's your alternatives that matter. That's how we make all of our decisions."[6]

Improving our thinking isn't just about having the answers to questions we've encountered before. It's not about memorizing a set of predetermined actions. It's not about relying on others to do the thinking for us. It's about delving deeper, beyond the surface level, and uncovering what lies hidden from our view.

Many people focus solely on what they stand to gain by choosing an option and forget to factor in what they stand to lose by forgoing another. But the ability to size up these costs is one of the things that separates great decision-makers from the rest.

One of my favorite examples of this is a story about Andrew Carnegie. When Carnegie was young and relatively inexperienced in his job at the Pennsylvania Railroad, there was a bad train wreck that left train cars strewn across the tracks and gridlocked the entire system. Carnegie's boss was absent, so Carnegie himself had to decide how to handle the event. Cleaning up the cars would save much of the cargo, but it would be a long and costly operation and would suspend all train traffic for days. Carnegie realized that a multiday systemwide shutdown wasn't worth the cost of the cargo and the cars. He sent a bold note signed in his boss's name: "Burn the cars!" When Carnegie's boss learned of his choice, he instantly made it the routine method of dealing with similar emergencies in the future.[7]

Thinking through opportunity costs is one of the most

effective things you can do in business and in life. The optimal way of exploring your options is to take all the relevant factors into account. You can't do this without considering opportunity costs.

There are two principles concerning opportunity costs. The first is this:

> **THE OPPORTUNITY-COST PRINCIPLE:** Consider what opportunities you're forgoing when you choose one option over another.

The second principle is closely related:

> **THE 3-LENS PRINCIPLE:** View opportunity costs through these three lenses: (1) Compared with what? (2) And then what? (3) At the expense of what?*

For most of us, the first lens is our default because the costs are direct and visible. For instance, think about purchasing a car. If you're like most people, you can narrow the decision down to a few options pretty quickly: "The Tesla will look extra cool and be fuel efficient, but will it be good for road trips? A BMW looks great and has more cargo space, but is a gas-powered vehicle behind the curve? Should I get the car that's $42,000 or $37,000?" When we compare the two models, we focus on what the additional $5,000 gets us in terms of features, and forget to view the choice through the other two lenses.

When we view the choice through the second lens, we consider the additional costs that will arise after we've selected an

---

* I got this from combining the ideas of Warren Buffett, Charlie Munger, and Peter Kaufman.

option—for example, how we'll need to charge the Tesla, its anticipated yearly operating costs, its durability, and how many long drives we'll go on annually. When we view the choice through the third lens, we consider what else we could do with that $5,000. Are we giving up a family vacation? What about the dividends we could get if we invested it? What about the savings if we pay down the mortgage? What about a rainy-day fund in case we lose our job? Looking through all three lenses helps us make a better decision.

Money is not the only opportunity cost to consider. It's just the most direct and visible, and for that reason people tend to focus on it. They convince themselves that what's easy to see is all that matters. But in many cases, the real value to thinking through opportunity costs is to understand the indirect hidden costs.

Time is not as easy to see as money but it's just as important. Suppose your family is growing, and it's time to move. Relocating to the suburbs will get you a bigger house with a bigger yard for the kids, and it'll be cheaper than buying a smaller duplex downtown with a backyard the size of a postage stamp. In this situation, many people think of how much money they'll save by moving to the suburbs, and get caught up in the happy thought of walking across the threshold of their new home for the first time. But this way of thinking views the situation through only the first lens. It doesn't disclose the less obvious costs of living in the suburbs. When we apply the other two lenses, we start seeing those costs more clearly.

Let's apply the second lens. Suppose you buy that house in the suburbs. Ask yourself, "And then what?" How will your circumstances change if you choose that option? For one thing, your commute might be different. Perhaps it goes from a predictable half hour each way to an unpredictable hour and a half.

Now apply the third lens. Ask yourself, "At the expense of what?" What are you not going to be able to do because you're spending an extra two to three hours a day in transit? Will you spend less time with your kids and your partner? What will you miss out on by not being with them? Will you be able to spend the commute learning a new language or reading some great literature, or will you have to deal with the frustration and stress of driving? Over time, which option is better for your mental and physical health?

> **TIP:** If you're having trouble assessing opportunity costs, it sometimes helps to put a price on them. For example, putting a price on those extra two to three hours a day spent commuting will make them more visible and easier to assess.

Keep in mind, though, that pricing things whose costs are difficult to assess is just a tool. Like any tool, it's useful for some jobs, but not useful for all. It's an attempt to make the invisible visible. Sometimes there are important factors that you simply can't put a price on without grossly distorting the trade-offs. As Einstein is thought to have said, "Not everything that can be counted counts, and not everything that counts can be counted." We'll see later on that assessing these "priceless" factors is something that the wisest decision-makers have mastered.

Evaluate the Options

YOU'VE WORKED OUT SOME POTENTIAL SOLUTIONS IN DE-tail. Each suggests a course of action that might work. You now need to evaluate the options and pick the one most likely to make the future easier. There are two components here: (1) your criteria for evaluating the options and (2) how you apply them.

Each problem has its own specific criteria. Some of the more common ones include opportunity cost, return on investment (ROI), and likelihood of the desired outcome, but there are many others. When you understand the problem, the criteria should be apparent. Recently I undertook a renovation. Some of my criteria included experience of the crew, availability, demonstrated pace on past projects, and quality of craftmanship.

If you find yourself struggling to determine specific criteria, it's a sign either that you don't really understand the problem, or that you don't understand the general features that criteria are supposed to have. Those features include the following:

Clarity: The criteria should be simple, clear, and free of any jargon. Ideally, you should be able to explain them to a twelve-year-old.

Goal promotion: The criteria must favor only those options that achieve the desired goal.

Decisiveness: The criteria must favor exactly one option; they can't result in a tie among several.

Criteria that fail to satisfy these conditions often lead to decision-making errors. When criteria are too complicated, people have trouble knowing how to apply them. When they are ambiguous, people have a green light to interpret them in whichever way suits them. As a result, people end up applying criteria in different ways based on what they want or how they feel at the moment. Their decision-making process becomes a playground for the emotion default.

When deciding at work, criteria that are ambiguous or jargon-laden lend themselves to endless debates as to their meaning. We assume that everyone has a shared understanding of what these words and phrases mean. They don't. We assume that our own definitions won't change. They might. What a word like "strategic" means to one person is often different from what it means to another. As a result, ambiguous criteria rob decision-makers of their ability to distinguish who's right from who's wrong, and force debates about semantics instead of which potential solution is the best.

Other times the criteria don't promote the goal. This is often the social default's doing. One common example is when leaders make decisions about hiring or promotion based not on someone's qualifications but on their likeable personality.

Being nice is not the same as being good at your job. Using niceness as a criterion in personnel decisions frequently doesn't promote the goals of the organization.

Sometimes criteria can promote the wrong goal—steering a team toward what it can do soonest, perhaps, instead of what's best for the company in the long run. A tragic example happened in January 1986.

The space shuttle *Challenger* was scheduled to take off in just a few short weeks. NASA had been trying to establish the space shuttle as a reliable way of conducting commercial and scientific missions in space, and adopted an incredibly ambitious launch schedule. NASA had coordinated with President Ronald Reagan to launch the shuttle the same day as his State of the Union address. The plan was for it to be a spectacular media event, with schools across the country lined up to receive their first science lessons from outer space.

But days before the launch, during a preflight meeting, engineers from Morton Thiokol, a contractor on the *Challenger* project, were shouting and in tears. They knew that the temperatures predicted for the date of the launch were likely too cold for the shuttle's O-rings to function successfully. If the O-rings failed, the result would be catastrophic. They wanted time to fix the problem or wait for warmer launch temperatures, and begged NASA to delay the launch. Their pleas were rejected. "I am appalled by your recommendation," one NASA official said. "When do you want me to launch? Next April?" said another.[1] Most of us who lived through the '80s remember what happened next; the *Challenger* exploded seventy-three seconds after taking off. The criteria for the launch date decision should obviously have been focused on promoting the goal of safety, not speed.

The inertia default can also inspire us to adopt criteria that aren't goal promoting. For example, upper management might fail to see that market conditions have changed. Rather than taking the time to understand the new conditions and adjust their criteria accordingly, they continue using the criteria they've used in the past even though those criteria aren't goal promoting in the present.

Criteria can also fail to be decisive. If they don't help you narrow the options, they're not useful. Indecisive criteria are another sign that you don't fully understand the problem and are operating out of fear that you'll be wrong. The social default preys on people who don't want to take responsibility for outcomes or who don't have clear ideas of what they want.

Think of choosing a restaurant for dinner with a group of friends. Someone will make an initial suggestion—like eating Mexican—and inevitably someone else will say, "I just had Mexican last night." Then you'll hear, "What about salads?" and someone will say, "I'm too hungry for salad." On and on ad nauseam: people say what they don't want until the group is so hungry they pick whatever is most convenient. I've seen this situation play out the same way so often it's comical. (Pay attention the next time it's happening to you!)

The problem here is that in many cases, purely negative criteria aren't decisive: they don't narrow the field of options down to one. As a result, people end up leaving the ultimate choice up to chance or circumstance. As the old saying goes, "If you don't know where you want to go, any road will take you there."

Suppose, by contrast, that when you and your friends were deciding where to eat, each of you stated not what you didn't want but rather what you did:

- "I want somewhere that serves salads within ten minutes' walking distance."
- "I want somewhere that serves burgers."
- "I really don't care; I just want to eat soon."

Making the decision would be much faster, and it would be more likely to get more people what they wanted.

Defining the Most Important Thing

Not all criteria are the same. There might be a hundred variables, but they are not equally important. When you're clear on what's important, evaluating options becomes easier. Many people are shy to pick out the most important thing because they don't want to be wrong.

When you don't communicate what's most important, people are left guessing about what matters. They need you to solve the problem for them. While you feel needed and important, you're also busy making all the decisions that your colleagues should be making.

A lot of managers secretly enjoy being the bottleneck. They like the way it feels when their team is dependent on them. Don't be fooled! This is the ego default at work, and it puts a ceiling on how far you will go. It tries to convince you that you're the best; that you're so smart, so skilled, so insightful that only you can make the decisions. In reality, you're just getting in the way of the team performing at its best.

I learned this lesson the hard way. I had just taken over a team and was surprised that they would check in with me before making any decisions—a pattern their previous manager had established.

To speed things up, I came up with a system for them to sort decisions into three boxes:

1. decisions they could make without any input from me,
2. decisions they could make after sharing their reasoning with me so I could double-check their judgment, and
3. decisions I wanted to make myself.

But the problem persisted.

After a few months, I consulted my mentor. "Do they know what decisions they should make and what decisions you want to make?" he asked. "Are the boxes clear?"

"Yes," I replied, "but due to the operational nature of our job, if I'm not around, they have to make decisions in the third box without me. That's where we're running into the biggest problems. They seem incapable of doing that."

"Do they know the one thing that's most important?" he probed.

"I'm not sure what you mean," I said. "What's most important differs for each decision." I listed off a few different types of decisions and how the variables were different.

"That's not what I mean," he replied. "Do they know what you value most?" I hesitated. He looked me square in the eye. "Shane, do *you* know what you value most?" I stared at him blankly. He sighed. "The problem isn't your team. It's you. You don't know what's most important. Until you do, your team will never make decisions without you. It's too risky for them to figure out the most important thing. Communicate that to your team, and they'll be able to make decisions on their own."

"What if they make the wrong decision?"

"As long as they make a decision based on the most important thing, they won't be wrong." He paused, then said slowly, "A lot of people reach their ceiling in this job because they can't figure out this one thing."

I learned three important lessons that day. First, I couldn't expect my team to make decisions on their own unless I told them how I wanted them to make those decisions. That meant focusing on the single most important thing and not inundating them with hundreds of variables to consider. Second, if they made the decision with the most important thing in mind, and it turned out wrong, I couldn't get upset with them. If I did that, they'd never make decisions without me. The third lesson was perhaps the most revealing: I myself didn't know what the most important thing was. That's why I couldn't tell them.

How to Safeguard the Evaluation Stage

There is only one most important thing in every project, goal, and company. If you have two or more most important things, you're not thinking clearly. This is an important aspect of leadership and problem-solving in general: you have to pick one criterion above all the others and communicate it in a way that your people can understand so they can make decisions on their own. This is true leadership. You need to be clear about what values people are to use when making decisions. If I tell you the most important thing is serving the customer, you know how to make decisions without me. If you make a bad judgment call, but it puts the customer first, I can't fault you. You did what I wanted.

But identifying what's most important is a skill. It takes practice. Here's how.

I recommend using sticky notes for this exercise. First, on each sticky note, write out one criterion—one thing that's important to you—in evaluating your options.

For example, before I decided to invest in Pixel Union—one of the largest and best design agencies in the Shopify universe—I wrote down some criteria that were important to me.

They included:

- A win-win for employees, customers, and shareholders
- Growing rather than shrinking the business
- Working with people I trust
- Not having to manage people or add more to my plate
- Not borrowing money
- A high probability of a decent return on investment

There are many more, but you get the idea. Place only one criterion on each sticky note because next, we're going to make your criteria battle.

Choose whichever criterion you think is the most important to you and place it on the wall. Then grab another criterion. Compare each and ask, "If I absolutely had to choose between only these two, which matters more?"

So to return to my example of investing in Pixel Union, the first battle might be this: earning a return on investment versus not having to manage people or add more to my plate.

If I could have only one of these—if either earning a return on my investment required managing people, or not managing people entailed making less money—which would it be? I'd choose earning more money even if it involved managing people. So I'd move that criterion higher.

Of course, I'd be willing to manage people only up to a point. If doing that became too time-consuming, I might have to reverse the order. That leads us to the next step: adding quantities. As your criteria battle one another, you'll find quantities make a difference. Add them to each criterion as they battle.

Suppose I find that I'm willing to spend five to ten additional hours per week managing people or being hands on, so long as my ROI is at least 15 percent per year. If I'd have to invest ten-plus hours per week, my ROI would have to be at least 20 percent per year, and if I'd have to invest twenty-plus hours per week, it would no longer be worth it to me—regardless of anticipated return—because of the opportunity cost of that time.

When you've finished ordering these two criteria, go to the next pair. Move from top to bottom, make your criteria battle one another for priority, and add the quantities that matter to you along the way.

When people do this exercise, they often look at a pair of criteria and think, "I don't necessarily have to choose between those two." Make them battle anyway! The point isn't really to compare them, it's to find out which one is more important. Maybe in real life you can satisfy both criteria—maybe, for instance, you can get a high ROI while investing in a socially responsible company, or you can get in shape while still eating out three times a week, or you can buy a house in a great location that fits your budget. But often, when we actually start pursuing an option, we find that we have to rank one criterion above another—even if only slightly. Most of the time, making your criteria battle is about calibrating shades of gray. It's a mental exercise that takes you out of reactive mode and moves you toward deliberative thinking.

Assigning quantitative values to your criteria often helps at this point. When you start comparing things and thinking how much you'll pay for them—and whether in a currency of time, money, collective brain power—you gain clarity about what matters most to you and what doesn't. You're forced to think in terms of benefits and risks, and you start to see things you didn't see before—previously invisible costs become visible. For all of these reasons, making your criteria battle moves you toward objectivity and accuracy, and helps reveal what you think is most important.

Once you've settled on your criteria and their order of importance, it's time to apply them to the options. Doing so requires that you have information about those options that meets two conditions: it's *relevant*, and it's *accurate*.

Most Information Is Irrelevant

When it comes to getting information that's relevant to the decision, remember this:

> **THE TARGETING PRINCIPLE:** Know what you're looking for before you start sorting through the data.

If you don't know what you're looking for, you're unlikely to find it, just as you're unlikely to hit the target if you don't know what you're aiming at. When you don't know what's important, you miss things that are relevant and spend a lot of time on things that are irrelevant.

Most information is irrelevant. Knowing what to ignore—separating the signal from the noise—is the key to not wasting valuable time. Think, for example, of investment decisions. The best investors know which variables probabilistically govern the outcomes, and they pay attention to those. They don't ignore everything else, but focusing primarily on those variables allows them to filter massive amounts of information very quickly.

People who can quickly distinguish what matters from what doesn't gain a huge advantage in a world where the flow of information never stops.

Knowing what to ignore allows you to focus on what matters. Follow the example of the best investors and know the variables that matter for evaluating the options *before* you start sorting through information.

Getting Accurate Information from the Source

When it comes to getting information that's accurate, there are two principles you should know: the HiFi Principle and the HiEx Principle. The first will help you find the best intel possible from within any given situation, and the second will help you find the best intel possible from outside of it.

> **THE HIFI PRINCIPLE:** Get high-fidelity (HiFi) information—information that's close to the source and unfiltered by other people's biases and interests.

The quality of your decisions is directly related to the quality of your thoughts. The quality of your thoughts is directly related to the quality of your information.

Many people treat all sources of information as if they're equally valid. They're not. While you might value getting everyone's opinion, that doesn't mean each opinion should be equally weighted or considered.

A lot of the information we consume is in the form of highlights, summaries, or distillations. It's the illusion of knowledge. We learn the answer but can't show our work.

Consider what happens when you consult a nutritionist. They take their years of experience and knowledge and compress it into a list of foods to eat and behaviors to implement. If you just want the answer, they will tell you what to eat and how much. This is an abstraction; it's like you're back in sixth-grade math class, copying answers from the person beside you. Sure, you got the right answer, but you don't know why it's the answer. You lack understanding, and information without understanding is dangerous.

It's natural to think these abstractions will save us time and improve our decision-making, but in many cases they don't. Reading a summary might be faster than reading a full document, but it misses a lot of details—details that weren't relevant to the person summarizing the information, but that might be relevant to you. You end up saving time at the cost of missing important information. Skimming inadvertently creates blind spots.

Information is food for the mind. What you put in today shapes your solutions tomorrow. And just as you are responsible for the food that goes into your mouth, you are responsible for the information that goes into your mind. You can't be healthy if you feed yourself junk food every day, and you can't make good decisions if you're consuming low-quality information. Higher quality inputs lead to higher quality outputs.

The desire for abstractions is understandable. The amount of information that bombards us daily can feel overwhelming. But the further the information is from the original source, the more filters it's been through before getting to you. Living on a diet of abstractions is like living on a diet of junk food: it has less nutritional value—less information content, which means you're not learning as much.

Real knowledge is earned, while abstractions are merely borrowed. Too often decision-makers get their information and observations from sources that are multiple degrees removed from the problem. Relying on these abstractions is a prime opportunity for the ego default to work its mischief. It conjures the illusion of knowledge: we feel confident about what to do without really understanding the problem.

You can't make good decisions with bad information. In fact, when you see people making decisions that don't make sense to you, chances are they're based on different information than you've consumed. Just as junk food eventually makes you unhealthy, bad inputs eventually produce bad decisions.

How do we get better information?

The person closest to the problem often has the most accurate information about it. What they tend to lack is a broader perspective. The person working on the line at McDonald's knows how to fix a recurring problem at their restaurant better than a person merely analyzing some data. What they don't know is how it fits into the bigger picture. They don't know whether the problem exists everywhere, or whether the solution would cause more harm than good if implemented globally, or how to roll the idea out to everyone.

My friend Tim Urban has a good metaphor to explain this concept. In the restaurant business, there are chefs and there are line cooks.[2] Both can follow a recipe. When things go according to plan, there is no difference in the process or the result. But when things go wrong, the chef knows why. The line cook often does not. The chef has cultivated depth of understanding through years of experience, experimentation, and reflection, and as a result, the chef, rather than the line cook, can diagnose problems when they arise.*

History shows that the greatest thinkers all used information

---

* This is also Nassim Taleb's idea of domain dependence: when we know the answer but lack the understanding to troubleshoot when things aren't working, or to apply our knowledge to problems that seem the same but aren't exactly the same.

that they collected personally. They earned their knowledge the hard way either in the trenches of experience or through careful study of exemplars. They looked for raw, unfiltered information, and ventured out into the world to interact with it directly.

Leonardo da Vinci is a great example. He kept journals throughout his life, and they contain notes about how he went about getting the right information. He wrote things like, "Get the master of arithmetic to show you how to square a triangle," and "Get a master of hydraulics to tell you how to repair a lock, canal and mill in the Lombard manner."

Great thinkers understand the importance of high-quality information, and that other people's abstractions are often limited in their usefulness.

As information travels up an organization, it tends to lose quality and nuance. Remember that children's game, telephone: you whisper a sentence to the next person, and that person whispers it to the next, and after it passes through half the class, the message is nothing like the original sentence. No single person necessarily changes it much, but the more people it passes through, the more all those little changes accumulate. The same thing happens when information travels through an organization. It goes through multiple filters, including individual levels of understanding, political interpretation, and biases. Details are abstracted from the original, and the signal is lost. The various incentives people have when they communicate information end up complicating things even further.

The problem isn't merely that people are unreliable transmitters of information; the problem is also that there are limitations on the information that abstractions can represent. Think of a road map. It's an abstract representation of a real landscape. That landscape includes rocks, plants, animals, cities, wind, and weather, along with many other things. We don't represent all of them when we map the landscape, only those things that interest us—for example, roads, rivers, and geographical boundaries. We pull these features away from the original and represent them in a way that makes them stand out. (That's in fact what the word "abstract" means: "to pull away from.")

Removing what doesn't serve our interests is what makes a map useful. But somewhere in the process, someone has decided what's useful and what isn't based on what interests them. What if we're interested in something else? What if we're interested in population densities or geological strata? A road map isn't designed to highlight these concepts, so it's not going to be very useful to us.

What's true of maps is true of any other abstractions: by nature, they're designed to serve the interests of their designers. If those designers don't have the same interests as you, their abstractions aren't going to give you the information you need. Similarly, any information you may get from a second-hand source has likely been filtered through that source's interests. Since your interests are likely different from theirs, their summaries, highlights, and descriptions are likely to leave out relevant information that could help you with your decision.

I learned the importance of accurate information while working for the CEO of a large company. Nothing crossed his desk without going through me first. Early one morning I saw an email from one of his direct reports flagging a technical problem that was affecting operations. After I told him what I'd heard about the problem, he asked a simple question: "Where did you get this information?" I replied that I'd heard it from the VP in charge of the division. The look on his face instantly turned to disappointment. Moments passed in silence.

Finally, he spoke softly, telling me that his decisions could only be as good as his information.

He wasn't getting the raw HiFi information. He knew that people in the organization had an incentive to convey things in a way that covered up mistakes or made themselves look good. And he knew that those filters would obscure rather than clarify the situation.

If you want to make better decisions, you need better information. Whenever possible, you need to learn something, see something, or do something for yourself. Sometimes the best information is the least transmissible.

HiFi Information Reveals Better Options

United States general George Marshall was a supremely competent and selfless leader. He never left the welfare of his troops to chance. He valued HiFi information and always went to the source.

At one point during World War II, the War Department ran into a difficult situation with the Air Force in the Pacific: pilots were refusing to fly. The reports Marshall received suggested there was something wrong with the planes. It wasn't a matter of parts. They were getting all the parts they were asking for. Marshall asked if the pilots wanted the planes modified in some way. The American planes were heavier and less maneuverable than the Japanese Zeros, so he had a plane stripped of its armor to reduce its weight. But that wasn't the problem. The pilots didn't want their planes stripped of armor.

Marshall struggled to understand what was going on. Talking to the commander gave him no insight, so he did what he often would: he sent someone "to look around and see things that weren't being reported—not just what they were yelling about."

No one likes the person sent from the head office to check on things—neither the commander nor the line cook. Everyone is suspicious. But Marshall needed eyes and ears on the ground to get to the heart of the matter. He knew he'd only get answers by going directly to the source.

What Marshall's direct report uncovered was that the Air Force ground crews didn't have any protection from mosquitoes. They had to work on the planes at night under electric lights, which attracted insects, and those mosquitoes were feasting on them. The mechanics had gotten so full of malaria or antimalarial medication that the pilots didn't trust their work and refused to fly.

The people back at headquarters, in mosquito-protected areas, had no idea what was really going on in the field. They were focused on combat supplies—ammunition, parts, food—but not mosquito netting. With his HiFi information, though, Marshall decided to override a portion of the tonnage they'd allocated for combat supplies and get those nets. Problem solved!

Marshall recognized that the only way to understand a problem and solve it was by going to the source. He constantly either went to the front lines himself or sent people he trusted to find out what was really going on.[3]

Making Sure You Get HiFi Information

Now that you understand the importance of HiFi information, here are the safeguards for ensuring you always get it.

SAFEGUARD: *Run an experiment.* Try something out to see what kinds of results it yields.

An experiment is a low-risk way of gathering important information. For example, if you want to know whether people will pay for something, try to sell it before you even create it. That's what my friends at Tuft & Needle did. They were one of the first companies to ship foam mattresses directly to consumers' homes. They shared an incredible story with me over coffee one day, about their early days. In order to validate their idea, they set up a landing page, bought some Facebook ads, and started taking orders. They didn't even have a product or a company yet; they just wanted to see if people would buy foam mattresses from them. After a few days of receiving orders, they had all the proof they needed that people would buy their product. They refunded all the orders and officially started their company. While this example may be a bit unorthodox, there are many ways in which experimenting can help determine whether there's sufficient demand for a product or service.

> **SAFEGUARD:** Evaluate the motivations and incentives of your sources. Remember that everyone sees things from a limited perspective.

Evaluating people's motivations and incentives is especially important when you don't have the ability to go and confirm something for yourself. If you absolutely must rely on someone else's information and opinions, you have a responsibility to think about the lens through which they view the situation. Everyone has a limited perspective into the problem. Everyone has a blind spot. It's your job as the decision-maker to weave their perspective together with others to get closer to reality.

A lot of what people consider information or fact is actually just opinion, or a few facts mixed with many opinions. For example, if you're looking to sell your house, everyone who's involved will have a different idea of what you'll make on the sale: the bank, your real estate agent, the buyer's agent, your friends, the home inspector, the internet, and the government. Each of them sees only part of the situation. Each has different motivations and incentives that shape how they see the world. To get a clearer picture of the concrete reality, consider how each person stands to benefit from the information they give you, and weave those perspectives together.

It helps to think of each person's perspective as a lens onto the world. When you put their glasses on, you see what they see and have better insight into what they might be feeling. But those glasses have blind spots, often missing important information or confusing fact with opinion. By trying on all the glasses, you see what others miss.

When you're getting information from other people, you need to keep an open mind. That means withholding your own judgment as long as possible. People often undermine the information-gathering process by subjecting others to their judgments, beliefs, and perspective. The point isn't to argue or disagree, however. Judging people and telling them they're wrong only shuts them down and prevents a free flow of information. When you're gathering information, your job is to see the world through other people's eyes. You're trying to understand their experience and how they processed it. You can learn valuable information even when you don't agree with their view of the world. Just ask questions, keep your thoughts to yourself, and remain curious about other perspectives.

SAFEGUARD: When you get information from other people, ask questions that yield detailed answers. Don't ask people what they think; instead, ask them *how* they think.

If you ask people what to do in a given situation, you might get the correct answer, but you haven't learned anything. Say a local government task force needs to hire a software developer for a project, but they have no experience doing so and don't know what to look for. Person A on the task force goes to a developer friend and asks, "Whom should I hire for this project?" Person B does the same but instead says, "I'm hiring a software developer, and I'd like to learn from your experiences. What skills matter and which ones can be learned on the job? Why? Where do I find the best people? How do I test these skills?" And so on.

Person B might not have a recommendation within the first conversation, but I'd give it ten-to-one odds that they find a better candidate in the end. The reason: Person B is asking about the principles that guide decision-making in this domain, not details about the specific case. They're asking others about their earned knowledge and making it their own.

Our goal in decision-making is not just to gather information, but to gather information relevant to our decision. That requires more than building an inventory of data points; it requires understanding the why and how behind those data points—the principles that good decision-makers use in this area.

Getting at those principles requires asking the right kinds of questions. There are three I'd recommend:

Question 1: What are the variables you'd use to make this decision if you were in my shoes? How do those variables relate to one another?

Question 2: What do you know about this problem that I (or other people) don't? What can you see based on your experience that someone without your experience can't? What do you know that most people miss?

Question 3: What would be your process for deciding if you were in my shoes? How would you go about doing it? (Or: How would you tell your mother/friend to go about doing it?)

Notice how different these questions are from the typical, "Here's my problem. What should I do?" Remember: the questions you ask help to determine the quality of the information you get.

Getting Accurate Information from Experts

We've talked about the importance of getting high-fidelity information. The second principle for getting accurate information is getting high-expertise information:

> **THE HiEX PRINCIPLE:** Get high-expertise (HiEx) information, which comes both from people with a lot of knowledge and/or experience in a specific area, and from people with knowledge and experience in many areas.

When someone close to the problem isn't available to you, look for people who recently solved a similar problem. The word "recent" is an important nuance here. When you want specific advice from an expert, look for someone who recently solved the problem you're trying to solve. Asking someone who solved your problem twenty years ago how they did it is not likely to offer specific and effective insights. You want a current expert—and no, I don't mean the talking heads on TV. They're rarely actual experts.

Experts can increase the accuracy of your information and decrease the time it takes to get it. Getting even one expert's advice can cut through a lot of confusion and help you quickly formulate and/or eliminate options.

I learned the value of expert advice firsthand when I began coding at an intelligence agency. It was a very different experience from coding as I'd learned it. In school, it was possible to basically just Google things and piece them together. People had solved these problems long ago and the solutions hadn't changed much. My job at the intelligence agency was much harder. Not only were we prohibited from Googling anything we were coding for security reasons, but even if we'd been allowed to, it wouldn't have helped: we were trying to do things no one had ever done before.

A few months in, I got stuck on a problem. Really stuck! As a kid I'd always taken in a lot of different perspectives on a problem, but in the end, I always thought if I just put my head down and worked harder, I'd figure it out eventually. Days went by. Then weeks. I couldn't understand what was happening. Finally, with my head down, I approached someone who had worked on a similar problem before and explained what I was stuck on.

"Let me look at your code," he said. In less than twenty minutes he diagnosed what was wrong: there was a subtle difference between what the documentation said would happen and what would actually happen in certain edge cases. Since most people wouldn't run into those edge cases, the problem wasn't documented anywhere. This person had faced and overcome the same problem, though, and it had taken him a long time to solve. He was happy to share his hard-earned knowledge. While I was a bit frustrated that I'd wasted weeks out of stubbornness, this exchange kick-started our relationship, and I learned a lot from him over the years.

Even one expert's opinion can be more helpful than the thoughts and guesses of dozens or hundreds of amateurs. But how do you recruit one to work with you?

I've experienced expert advice from both sides: getting and giving. I reach out to experts all the time for insight, and I have thousands of people who reach out to me for advice. Let me share what I've learned on both recruiting experts and working with them.

Getting Experts on Your Side

Many people don't want to reach out to experts for help, either because they don't think it's an option, or because they're afraid of being a nuisance. Sometimes, if we know the expert, we're embarrassed. Maybe they'll discover we know less than we actually do!

If you have any anxieties of this sort, the first thing to understand is that experts *love* sharing what they've learned when they know it'll make a difference. Helping others achieve their goals is one of the things that make life and work meaningful. To put it in perspective, think of a time in your life when someone asked you for help on something you excel at, and you came through for them. How did it feel? For most of us, sharing expertise feels pretty good. We enjoy exercising an ability we have, and we also enjoy gaining recognition for having it.

Experts don't treat all requests for help equally, though. Some requests really don't feel good to receive. Usually these are requests of the tell-me-what-I-should-do type. Often these people haven't done the work ahead of time, they just want you to decide for them. I get hundreds—if not thousands—of these requests a year. People want me to solve their problems for them. They send twenty pages of thoughts and say, "What should I do?"*

Remember: the goal isn't to have someone tell you what to do; rather, it's to learn how an expert thinks about the problem, which variables they consider relevant, and how those variables interact over time. If you present a problem, and an expert simply tells you what to do, they're just giving you an abstraction. You might get the answer right, but you haven't learned anything. And if things go wrong, which they inevitably will, you won't have a clue as to why. You're the line cook masquerading as the chef. If you ask them *how* they think about the problem, that's when you start deepening your understanding.

So let's talk about how to approach an expert in a way that will set your request apart and get people excited to help you. Here are five tips:

- **Show that you have skin in the game:** When you reach out to an expert, make them aware of the time, energy, and money you've already invested in the problem. Let them know you've done the work and that you're stuck. When I see requests from someone who shows they're invested in solving a problem, and who demonstrates they've done their research to craft a pitch around a very specific issue I can help with, I'm happy and eager to respond. Contrast that with emails that say, "Hey Shane, what do you think of this investment opportunity?" Which would you be more excited to answer?

---

*Please note, this never works. If you can't offer value and get your point across in a few sentences, you won't even get read.

- **Get precise on your ask:** Be very clear what you're looking for. Are you looking for them to review your plan and provide feedback? Are you looking for them to introduce you to people who can solve the problem? Whatever it is that you want, just be clear.

- **Show respect for their time and energy:** Explicitly stating that the person you're reaching out to is an expert whose time and energy you respect goes a long way to secure their goodwill. You should also demonstrate your respect for them, though. For instance, do not ask for fifteen minutes to pick their brain; instead, ask if they offer one-off consulting sessions and how much they charge for them. Experts are expensive and most of the time for good reason. If you're paying $1,000 to $2,000 per hour for something, it forces you to get clear on what you want before you hop on the call. Paying for someone's time not only compensates them for the value they bring to the table but forces you to make sure you're not mumbling through the call and wasting their time and yours.

- **Ask for their reasons and listen:** As mentioned previously, don't just ask experts what they think, ask them how they think. Use them as a resource to train yourself how to evaluate things so that you can start embodying an expert way of operating. You don't have to agree with what they're saying, but remember: your goal is to learn from them how to think better, not to have them solve your problem for you.

- **Follow up:** If you want to build a network and make this more than a transactional request, follow up to report on your progress no matter what the outcome is. Whether their advice helped you in this case or not, following up and keeping them updated on your progress primes them to help you in the future. When they see that you took their advice seriously, they're going to want to help you again.

Of course, most experts aren't able to respond to everyone who needs their help. It's much easier if you develop a personal relationship with people before you need their help. That way the request isn't purely transactional. It's impossible to predict which fields you might someday need an expert in, but that's one reason to cast a wide net socially and professionally. I just looked at my inbox last week and had fifty-three requests for "help" in one form or another. Two were from friends. I can't reply to them all, so where do you think my time will go?

Experts vs. Imitators

Getting HiEx information requires that you get help from real experts. But there are many people who claim to be experts (or whom other people claim to be experts) who really aren't.

> **SAFEGUARD:** *Take time to distinguish real experts from imitators.* Not everyone who claims to be an expert is. Take the time to know the difference.

Think of all the money managers who borrow their talking points from Warren Buffett. They might sound like Buffett, but they don't know how to invest the way Buffett does. They're imitators. Charlie Munger once commented on this: "It's very hard to tell the difference between a good money manager and someone who just has the patter down."

But what if you're not an expert yourself? How do you tell the difference between an expert and an imitator?

Experts are usually enthusiastic about their area of expertise. That's why they're good at it: they spend even their spare time mastering and refining their knowledge and skills, and it shows. Imitators are less concerned with being great and more concerned with looking great. That concern makes it easy for the ego to take over.

Here are some things to look for:

- **Imitators can't answer questions at a deeper level.** Specific knowledge is earned, not learned, so imitators don't fully understand the ideas they're talking about.* Their knowledge is shallow. As a result, when you ask about details, or first principles or nonstandard cases, they don't have good answers.
- **Imitators can't adapt their vocabulary.** They can explain things using only the vocabulary they were taught, which is often full of jargon. Because they don't fully understand the ideas behind the vocabulary, they can't adapt the way they talk about those ideas to express them more clearly to their audience.
- **Imitators get frustrated when you say you don't understand.** That frustration is a result of being overly concerned with the appearance of expertise—which they might not be able to maintain if they have to really get into the weeds with an explanation. Real experts have earned their expertise and are excited about trying to share what they know. They aren't frustrated by your lack of understanding; they instead love your genuine curiosity about something they care about.

---

* This is a play on a quote by Naval Ravikant. "Specific knowledge cannot be taught, but it can be learned" (@naval), Twitter, January 17, 2019, 10:48 p.m., https://twitter.com/naval/status/1086108038539309061.

- **Experts can tell you all the ways they've failed.** They know and accept that some form of failure is often part of the learning process. Imitators, however, are less likely to own up to mistakes because they're afraid it will tarnish the image they're trying to project.

- **Imitators don't know the limits of their expertise.** Experts know what they know, and also know what they don't know. They understand that their understanding has boundaries, and they're able to tell you when they're approaching the limits of their circle of competence. Imitators can't. They can't tell when they're crossing the boundary into things they don't understand.

A final note on distinguishing experts from imitators: Many of us learn about a subject not by reading original research or listening to the expert for hours, but by reading something intended to be highly transmissible. Think again of the difference between reading an academic article and reading a newspaper article about it. While they know more than the layman, popularizers are not experts themselves. Instead, they are good at clearly and memorably communicating ideas. As a result, popularizers often get mistaken for experts. Keep that in mind when you're in the market for an expert: the person with real expertise is often not the person who made the subject popular.

Do it!

YOU'VE CONSIDERED THE OPTIONS. YOU'VE EVALUATED them. You've found the best. It's time to act!

There is no purpose to knowing what you should do and not doing it. If you want results, you need action.

Making a judgment and executing it is easier than it seems and harder than others imagine. One reason we fail to take action is that we're scared to deal with the consequences. It's not so much that we don't know what to do as much as we don't want to deal with the reality of doing it. We don't want to have conversations, because they might hurt people's feelings. We don't want to fire the person that we like, even though we know they're wrong for the job.

Our ego conspires with the social default and the inertia default to weaken our resolve and keep us from doing what we need to do. But that's not the only reason we fail to act.

Another big reason we find action hard is that we're afraid of being wrong. In this case inertia holds us in place as we gather more and more information in the false hope that we can ultimately eliminate uncertainty.

There are three principles that can help you know when to stop deliberating and start acting. But first, let's discuss a helpful way of categorizing decisions by considering how *consequential* they are, and how *reversible* they are.

Consequentiality and Reversibility

Consequential decisions affect the things that matter most: whom you marry, where you live, which business you launch. The more a decision affects what matters to you—either in the short term or the long term—the more consequential it is.

Reversible decisions can be undone by a later course of action. The harder or more costly it is to undo a decision's effects, the less reversible it is. It's easy to eat a chocolate bar, but once you've eaten it, it's done. You can't undo it. Having a baby is the same. Once you have one, you can't undo it (nor would you want to!). At the other extreme would be a decision whose effects cost nothing to undo. I can decide to sign up for a free fourteen-day trial of something, knowing full well it's easy to undo.

We can represent different kinds of decisions in terms of their degrees of consequence and reversibility on a graph (see the following figure). Among these decisions, two types deserve special attention: decisions that are highly consequential and irreversible, and decisions that are inconsequential and highly reversible.

When a decision is highly consequential and irreversible, its effects ripple throughout your life, and there's no way to stop them. Some people call these "lead dominoes."

When decisions are like lead dominoes, the cost of a mistake is high. Exactly the opposite is true of a decision that's inconsequential and easily reversed. The cost of a mistake is

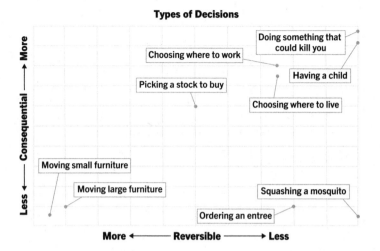

Types of Decisions

low: if you don't like the outcome, you can just reverse it. The biggest mistake in cases like these is wasting time and mental energy. If you can take something back, or it doesn't really matter, continuing to gather information becomes a drain on resources.

If you've ever bought a mattress, you'll know exactly what I mean. You spend hours—if not days—looking at mattresses, reading reviews, comparing prices, and considering whether you're a hot or cold sleeper. You finally decide on a mattress, and have it delivered, only to find that it isn't what you dreamed of. So you exchange it for your fallback option anyway. You could have saved hours or days simply ensuring the store had a flexible return policy, deciding on a mattress within an hour, and moving on. When the cost of a mistake is low, move fast.

Three Principles for Action

Now that we have a way of categorizing decisions by their degrees of consequence and revisability, let's talk about some principles. The first is this:

> **THE ASAP PRINCIPLE:** If the cost to undo the decision is low, make it as soon as possible.

In fact, if something is too inconsequential, then engaging in *any* decision-making might be a waste. Just choose. Decide quickly, and learn by doing. You'll save time, energy, and resources that you can use for decisions that really matter.

If, on the other hand, the decision is highly consequential and irreversible, then the stakes are high. The biggest risk here is moving too fast and missing something important. You want to gather as much information as you can before deciding. Therefore, the second principle is:

> **THE ALAP PRINCIPLE:** If the cost to undo a decision is high, make it as late as possible.

Remember to factor the cost of analysis into your decisions. This is something many people fail to do. Most decisions require an art that balances speed and accuracy. When you move too slowly on small decisions, you waste time and energy, no matter how accurate you may be. When you go too fast, you miss crucial information, make assumptions, overlook the basics, rush to judgment, and often solve the wrong problem. When things are hectic, however—even when speed matters—you need to slow down, just a little.

Michael Lewis gives an example of this in *The Undoing Project* about a woman who crashed head on into another car.[1] Medics rushed her to Sunnybrook Hospital, which is located next to Canada's busiest stretch of highway. Sunnybrook had a reputation for treating the emergencies and traumas that come from car crashes, yet the woman had so many broken bones, the physicians missed some. Don Redelmeier was the Sunnybrook epidemiologist. His job was to "check the understanding of the specialists for mental errors." He was there, in other words, to check other people's thinking. "Wherever there is uncertainty there has got to be judgment," said Redelmeier, "and wherever there is judgment there is an opportunity for human fallibility." Doctors may be experts, but they're still human, still fallible, and to complicate things further, their patients often give them unreliable information.

When things move fast, and life-and-death decisions need to be made, we often see only the things we're specifically trained to see, and miss others that are nevertheless relevant. In this case, the woman presented another problem beyond all the broken bones: her heartbeat was highly irregular. Before she lost consciousness, she mentioned a history of an overactive thyroid, which is a classic cause of an irregular heartbeat.

Redelmeier entered as the team looking after her was preparing to administer the drugs for hyperthyroidism: "[He] asked everyone to slow down. To wait. Just a moment. Just to check their thinking—and to make sure they were not trying to force the facts into an easy, coherent, but ultimately false story."

He wanted to slow things down because they had leaped to a conclusion that seemed to fit without considering other reasons: "Hyperthyroidism is a classic cause of an irregular heart rhythm, but hyperthyroidism is an infrequent cause of an irregular heart rhythm," he would say later. While it fit, it was unlikely—possible but not probable.

The staff began searching for other causes, and quickly determined she had a collapsed lung. "Like her fractured ribs, her collapsed lung had failed to turn up on the X-ray. Unlike the fractured ribs, it could kill her." They ignored the thyroid and treated the collapsed lung, and her heartbeat returned to normal. When her official thyroid tests came back the next day, they were normal. As Redelmeier said, "You need to be so careful when there is one simple diagnosis that instantly pops into your mind that beautifully explains everything all at once. That's when you need to stop and check your thinking."

When the stakes are high, and there are no take-backs, you want to decide at the last moment possible, and keep as many options on the table as you can while continuing to gather information.

In driver's education, we learn that when you're on the freeway driving at high speeds, you need to keep a pocket open in front of you in case someone unexpectedly veers into your lane or stops abruptly. Keeping extra distance between cars allows you to keep options open for whatever might happen. This is the same reason you should wait as long as possible when making an important decision. You want to give yourself as many options in the future so that if something changes, you have the space to maneuver and reposition yourself along the path of greatest opportunity.

How do you know when it's finally time to act?

When the cost of failure is cheap, the speed at which you come to a decision matters as much as the decision itself. When failure is expensive, it makes sense to learn more before taking action.

Defaults can transform caution into an excuse not to act if

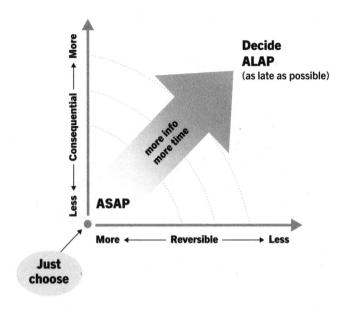

you don't resist them. Anyone who has held on to a failing job, relationship, or investment too long knows that information gathering reaches a point of diminishing returns—at some point the cost of getting more information is exceeded by the cost of losing time or opportunity.

A friend of mine works with engineers. He says they tend to be highly risk averse: they wait as long as possible to decide and can't tell when they should act more quickly. "They keep thinking that gathering more data will make things firmer," he said, "but they've already been prototyping and gathering information for months. They don't know when to stop and commit. They start losing interest in the problem too, because all they're doing is having meetings, aligning, gathering information, and writing up a giant document laying out how they made their decision. They're all aware of basic decision-making skills, but they really, really struggle to know when enough is enough." And it's not just engineers.

Decision-makers at large have become increasingly susceptible to analysis paralysis because so much data has become available to them. If you've ever struggled with analysis paralysis, a third principle can help you know when to stop deliberating and start acting:

> **THE STOP, FLOP, KNOW PRINCIPLE:** Stop gathering more information and execute your decision when either you Stop gathering useful information, you First Lose an OPportunity (FLOP), or you come to Know something that makes it evident what option you should choose.

Let's consider the Stop, FLOP, and Know conditions one at a time.

First, when you've stopped gathering useful information, it's time to act. More information isn't always better, and there are signs that you've gathered enough. When I interviewed *The Princeton Review* co-founder Adam Robinson,[2] for instance, he told me about a seminal study done by a psychologist named Paul Slovic back in 1974 that illustrates the folly of gathering too much information.

Slovic put eight horse handicappers in the same room and told them he wanted to see how well they could predict the winners of forty horse races, over four rounds of ten races each. In the first round each handicapper was given any five pieces of information he wanted on each horse. One handicapper might want the height and weight of the jockey; another might want the highest finish a horse had ever had. The handicappers also had to state how confident they were in their predictions.

At the end of the first round, with only five pieces of information, they were 17 percent accurate. Given there were ten horses to a race, they were 70 percent better than the 10 percent chance they'd have with zero information. They were 19 percent confident in their predictions, which isn't too far from their actual results.

Each round gave them more and more information. For round two they were given ten pieces of information, then twenty in round three, and forty in the fourth and final round.

In the final round, they were still only 17 percent accurate. The thirty-five additional pieces of information did, however, move their confidence level to 34 percent. All of the extra information made them no more accurate but a lot more confident.

Confidence increases faster than accuracy. "The trouble with too much information," Robinson told me, "is you can't reason with it." It only feeds confirmation bias. We ignore additional information that doesn't agree with our assessment, and gain confidence from additional information that does.

In my life and in the lives of people I've worked with, these are some signs you've hit the limit of useful information you can gather:

- You are able to argue credibly for and against the options you're considering from all angles.
- You're stretching for insight by asking people for advice who are more than one step removed from the problem or who don't have experience solving problems of this sort.
- You feel like you need to learn more, but you've stopped learning new things, and are instead in a constant loop reviewing the same information (or same arguments) over and over.

When you've hit any of these points, you've probably gotten all the useful information you're going to get. It's time to decide. That's Stop, now let's move on to FLOP.

If you're facing a highly consequential and irreversible decision, and you're waiting as long as possible to make up your mind, the time to decide is when you start losing opportunities. For example, if you're selling a house, you might want to wait as long as possible to actually sell it. You go as far as listing it, setting a price, and getting offers, but when buyers start walking away, or you're about to break a legal contract, then you're starting to lose options, and it's time to act.

Likewise, suppose your partner wants to take your relationship to the next level—be it going exclusive, living together, or getting engaged. Those are big defining moments in your relationship, and if you're unsure, it makes sense to take your time deciding. But eventually your partner is going to get fed up and walk away. Right before that happens, when your partner makes it clear that you're on the threshold of losing options, it's time to decide.

Remember, the rationale behind the ALAP Principle is to preserve optionality. When options start diminishing, it's time to act using whatever information you have. That's FLOP: if you're waiting to decide, wait no longer than your First Lost Opportunity.

It's finally time to act when you come to know something that makes it clear what you should do. Sometimes you gather a critical piece of information that makes your decision easy, perhaps a First Lost Opportunity. Other times, especially in more ambiguous situations like relationships, it's just a gut feeling that doesn't go away or change. Either way, there's always a moment when you simply know at a core level exactly what to do.

Knowing what to do isn't enough, though. You have to take action.

Do it!

Margin of Safety

YOU DON'T ALWAYS NEED TO HAVE THE ULTIMATE SOLU-
tion to make progress. If it remains unclear which path is best,
often the next best step is just to eliminate paths that lead to
outcomes you don't want. Avoiding the worst outcomes main-
tains optionality and keeps you moving forward.

Sometimes things fail for reasons beyond our control. A
lot of tricky and highly consequential decisions, though, fail
for preventable reasons. When we don't consider how things
might go wrong and plan for them in advance, we're left flat-
footed when they do go wrong. Then we end up reacting instead of reasoning. It's much easier to plan for things that
could go wrong in advance when you're calm and open-minded
than it is to respond when things are in the midst of going
wrong.

When failure is expensive, it's worth investing in large margins of safety.

If you're an investor, you've likely heard the story of Long-
Term Capital Management (LTCM), a hedge fund founded in
1994 by a prominent investor who managed to get two Nobel

laureates on his board. LTCM had a high risk portfolio that was highly acclaimed for its incredible returns—over 21 percent in its first year, then 43 percent in its second year, and 41 percent in its third year.

Imagine being an investor in this environment. You see this hedge fund taking off, and your friends are boasting of their success and urging you to join in on the bonanza. They tell you about the amazing people working there—people with incredibly high IQs, including two Nobel Prize winners, who are also experienced in their respective fields and who have invested substantial amounts of their own money.

You watch your friends double and then quadruple their investments. You start wondering whether you should invest everything as well. Your own portfolio is returning 8 to 12 percent year over year—good returns, but not 40 percent! Is the rest of the world going to get rich while you play it safe?

Consider now two scenarios. In the first, you decide to follow your friends and invest everything you have in the fund. A few months later, Asia and Russia experience a financial crisis. That crisis together with LTCM's highly leveraged investments loses them $4.6 billion in less than four months. The chart on the next page shows what that loss would look like if you had invested $1,000 from the beginning in 1994. In this scenario, you (and your friends) end up in financial ruin.

Imagine now a different scenario. It's November 1997. You just hit the peak of returns at LTCM. If you anticipate that the future is going to be different from the past, you probably won't assume astronomical losses, and might invest a little. But if you're wise, you'll maintain a margin of safety.

A margin of safety is a buffer between what you expect to happen and what could happen. It's designed to save you when surprises are expensive.

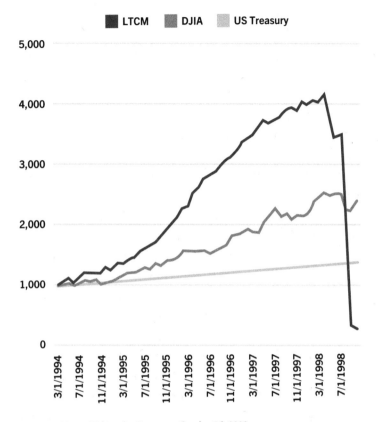

Source: Jay Henry, Wikimedia Commons, October 26, 2009

A margin of safety is like having insurance. If you know in advance you won't need to make a claim this year, it's a waste of money to buy insurance. The problem is that you don't know in what year you'll need to make a claim, so you buy it every year. It might seem like a waste of money in years when nothing happens, but it shows its real value in years when something does.

Building a margin of safety means giving yourself as much cushioning and coverage in the future as possible. It's a way of preparing yourself for the widest range of possible future outcomes—and protecting yourself against the worst ones. In the second scenario, for instance, you can prepare yourself for the various bad outcomes that 1998 might bring by investing only one tenth of your portfolio in the fund. As a result, when the 1998 financial crisis comes, you'll lose at most 10 percent of your investments. That won't leave you happy, but it won't leave you financially ruined either.

Your defaults are hard at work in the first scenario—not just the social default that convinces you that you're better off following the crowd, but the ego default as well. It convinces you that you don't need a margin of safety, because you know what's going to happen. You feel confident predicting the future—predicting that the future is going to be like the past, that LTCM's fourth year is going to be like its first three. The problem is that tomorrow is never exactly like today, and in that fourth year, the plan that garnered LTCM's success in the previous three years stops working.

In the second scenario, your decision isn't based on a prediction; it's instead prepared for a future in which your best-case scenario might not materialize. It's that preparation mindset—as opposed to a prediction mindset—that saves you in the second scenario.

Warren Buffett has a saying that I often come back to: "Diversification is protection against ignorance. It makes little sense if you know what you are doing."[1] The thing is, most of us rarely know what we are doing with the confidence required to go all in. When you don't know what you are doing, a margin of safety saves you from the worst outcomes. Even when you do know what you're doing and you make the best possible decision at the time, things can change.

If the worst-case outcomes never come to pass, the margin

of safety will appear like a waste. The minute you convince yourself you could have done better without a margin of safety is exactly when you need it most.

We can't prepare for everything. Some horrific events defy imagination, and no amount of preparation can ever give you enough optionality to deal with them. Yet we know from history that there are certain unfortunate events that we're guaranteed to experience and that we can in fact prepare for, even if we have no idea when they'll arrive. On a personal level, these include:

- Grief from losing a loved one
- Health issues
- Relationship changes
- Financial pressures
- Challenges in meeting our career goals

On a more macro level, they include the following:

- War and political dissent
- Natural disasters
- Environmental and ecological changes
- Economic fluctuations: both collapse and growth
- Technological advances and resistance to them

How do you build a margin of safety?

Let's start with a very typical application. Engineers build margins of safety into everything they design. Suppose, for instance, that we're designing a bridge and calculate that on an average day it will need to support 5,000 tons at any one time.

If we build it to withstand 5,001 tons, we have no margin of safety: What if there's heavier traffic than usual one day?

What if our calculations and estimates are a little off? What if the material weakens over time at a rate faster than we imagined? To account for all of these contingencies, we'd need to design the bridge to withstand 10,000 or even 20,000 tons. Why? Because we don't know what the future will bring. We don't know whether multiple trucks will ever get stuck on the bridge at the same time. We don't know whether vehicles in the future will be much heavier than they are now. We don't know many things about the future. So we design the bridge in a way that protects travelers in the widest range of possible future outcomes.

Keep in mind as you're preparing for the future that the worst outcomes in history have always surprised people at the time. You can't use the historical worst case as your baseline. Engineers don't rely just on the historical use of current bridges. You have to really stretch your imagination to explore and anticipate what could potentially go wrong.

Here's a simple heuristic for creating a margin of safety so you know when "enough is enough."

> **TIP:** The margin of safety is often sufficient when it can absorb double the worst-case scenario. So the baseline for a margin of safety is one that could withstand twice the amount of problems that would cause a crisis, or maintain twice the amount of resources needed to rebuild after a crisis.

For example, if you want to feel financially secure even if you lose your job, you can estimate how long it will take you to gain employment again, and then save enough to live off savings for double that amount of time.

That's our baseline. But we need to adapt our margin of

safety to the individual and situational circumstances. If the cost of failure is high, and outcomes are more consequential, you want a large margin of safety. For instance, if you're worried about losing your job, and you're in a sector or economy that's volatile, you'll want to increase the length of time you can take care of yourself while unemployed.

If the cost of failure is low, and outcomes are less consequential, you can often reduce or skip the margin of safety. The longer something exists and performs well, the higher the probability that its pattern of success will continue. Coca-Cola isn't going anywhere in the near future; neither is Johnson & Johnson.

Yet even established patterns aren't foolproof. As Nassim Taleb writes in *The Black Swan*, "Consider a turkey that is fed every day. Every single feeding will firm up the bird's belief that it is the general rule of life to be fed every day by friendly members of the human race 'looking out for its best interests,' as a politician would say. On the afternoon of the Wednesday before Thanksgiving, something unexpected will happen to the turkey. It will incur a revision of belief." Our outcomes can sometimes upend even our most well-established expectations.

However, if you have a lot of expertise and data, you can reduce your margin of safety yet further. Here's an example: Warren Buffett aims to buy stocks that are 30–50 percent less than their true value. So he has a 30–50 percent margin of safety on stocks. But he'll pay close to a dollar on the dollar for stocks that he understands well. So there's only maybe a 20 percent margin of safety on the stocks he's the most confident in.

One of Warren Buffett's core tenets for buying a business is that if he doesn't understand it, he doesn't buy it. In other words, if he doesn't have enough information to calculate a margin of safety, he doesn't invest at all. He also knows that not all margins of safety will protect him—the goal isn't to get it perfect for every stock he buys; it's to use the best possible strategy for all his stocks in the big picture.

Here's the bottom line: Predicting the future is harder than it seems. Things are great until they're not. If things are good, a margin of safety seems like a waste. When things go wrong, though, you can't live without it. You need a margin of safety most at the very moment you start to think you don't.

Bullets before Cannonballs

If you're still gathering information, don't get overinvested in just one option. Keep your future options open by taking small, low-risk steps toward as many options as possible before committing everything to just one.

When you're gathering information about your options, your best bet is to gather as much information as possible about each without investing too much time, money, or energy in any particular one. In *Great by Choice*, Morten Hansen and Jim Collins call this approach shooting bullets before cannon-balls:[2]

> Picture yourself at sea, a hostile ship bearing down on you. You have a limited amount of gunpowder. You take all your gunpowder and use it to fire a big cannon-ball. The cannonball flies out over the ocean . . . and misses the target, off by 40 degrees. You turn to your stockpile and discover that you're out of gunpowder. You die.
>
> But suppose instead that when you see the ship bearing down, you take a little bit of gunpowder and fire a bullet. It misses by 40 degrees. You make another bullet

and fire. It misses by 30 degrees. You make a third bullet and fire, missing by only 10 degrees. The next bullet hits—ping!—the hull of the oncoming ship. Now, you take all the remaining gunpowder and fire a big cannonball along the same line of sight, which sinks the enemy ship. You live.[3]

Here's an example of bullets before cannonballs that I witnessed in real life. A client of mine—we'll call him Solomon—was looking to hire someone to run his manufacturing business so he could step down and pursue other opportunities. He tried twice to choose a CEO to replace him. But each time, while the candidate looked great on paper, they didn't work out in practice.

I recommended that instead of investing heavily in one candidate and turning down others, he should have two or three candidates perform a small test project lasting a couple weeks. These small simultaneous tests would maintain his optionality, and seeing the candidates perform in real life would be magnitudes more insightful than interviewing them or reading their résumés.

The two candidates were paid well for their time and tasked with a project that required them to work with the team to understand the problem, gather information, and chart a course forward.

The plan worked, and it yielded a surprising result: the candidate with the less impressive résumé was far and away the best with the team and made recommendations that ended up saving Solomon's company more than they'd paid for the project. More importantly, if neither of the candidates had worked out, the company wasn't saddled with an expensive exit cost.

Performing small, low-risk experiments on multiple options—in other words, shooting bullets and calibrating—keeps your options open before you commit the bulk of your resources to shooting a cannonball. Thinking about medical school? Shadow a doctor or a resident for a day. Take the MCAT and see what you score, or apply to colleges and see where you're accepted. Thinking about a new career? Try doing it freelance a few nights per week first. Thinking about launching a new product? See if people are willing to pay for it before you build it.

Preserving options carries a cost and can make you feel like you're missing out. It's hard watching others take action sometimes, even when those actions don't make sense for you. Don't be fooled! This is the social default at work. It tempts you to feel like it's okay to fail so long as you're part of the crowd.

While some people are quick to join the crowd, others prefer to be correct. Preserving optionality can make you look stupid in the short term, which means that from time to time you'll have to tolerate people treating you like you're a fool. But if you look at the most successful people in the world, they've all looked short-term stupid on a number of occasions, when they were keeping their options open and waiting for the right time to act.

Warren Buffett sat out most of the dot-com craze of the late '90s, and appeared to miss the stampeding bull market that came with it. People began chattering that he'd lost his touch. He may have looked stupid to some speculators for a few years—until the tech bubble burst and he still had tremendous cash reserves.

Live with a Decision before Announcing It

Have you ever spent time crafting an email, and then instantly regretted it as soon as you hit "Send"? I have. It's one of the worst feelings in the world. Perhaps not as bad, though, as announcing a major decision too soon and then realizing it was a mistake.

Many leaders want to announce a decision the moment they've made it. This is natural: they want to show others how decisive they are, and let everyone else revel in their dazzling new venture. But announcing right away can be like the email you can't unsend. It starts things moving, and makes changing your mind much harder. That's why I created a rule for myself: I make major decisions and then sleep on them before telling anyone.*

However, it turned out that sleeping on decisions by itself wasn't enough. I added another element to the rule: before going to bed, I would write a note to myself explaining why I'd made the decision. Doing so allowed me to make the invisible visible. When I woke up in the morning, I'd read the note. More often than I'd like to admit, my best thinking from the day before fell short upon inspection in the harsh light of the morning. Sometimes I'd realize I really didn't understand the problem as well as I thought I did. Other times, it just didn't feel right anymore. And I've come to learn that this feeling is important to explore.

Living with a decision before announcing it allows you to look at it from a new perspective and verify your assumptions. Once you've made the decision—even if you haven't communi-

---

*I got the phrase "live with the decision" from a conversation with Randall Stutman, who has taught me so many of the lessons in this book.

cated it—you start seeing things in a new light.* Your brain processes all the potential results of the decision as though it had already been made and put into action. This can often help you see nuances you might have missed, and those might, in turn, change how you implement the decision. Maybe you're promoting someone, and you're worried about their ability to lead a meeting and organize a team. Living with the decision might spur you to have them organize a meeting, see what happens, and recalibrate if necessary.

Also, living with a decision on your own for a day—or even two—allows you to check it with your emotions. Does this decision feel good in your bones? Do your brain and your heart and your guts all agree with it? Most decisions will feel fine. But a handful won't. If one doesn't feel right, it's a sign that something is off, and you need to dig deeper before announcing your decision. Keeping it to yourself before executing allows you to keep open the possibility of undoing it.

The Fail-Safe Principle

Implementing fail-safes will help ensure that your decision is executed according to plan.

Imagine standing on Mount Everest, just fifty meters from reaching the very top. Your entire body is aching. Your mind is numb. It feels like no matter how hard you breathe there's just not enough oxygen. You've been training for years, spent $60,000 on guides and travel, sacrificing time with your family and friends in the process. You've told everyone today is the day you'll make the attempt. Everything you've worked for is

---

*As Randall Stutman taught me, if you walk around like you've already made the decision, you start to filter all new information through the lens of having already made the decision.

right in front of you. You can see your goal. You're nearly there. But you're thirty minutes behind schedule, and oxygen is running low. Do you turn around or push forward?

The world's best Sherpas know that the most dangerous part of summiting Mount Everest isn't reaching the peak; it's the descent. So much energy is spent getting to the top that even if climbers are running out of strength or oxygen, they keep pushing themselves to the summit. They spend so much of their resources getting there, they neglect to account for the ordeal of getting back. Lost in "summit fever" they forget that the most important thing isn't making it to the top, but making it home. You can't win, after all, if you don't survive.

For those of us outside the situation, likely with no plans to climb Everest, the idea of summit fever seems a bit ridiculous: reaching the summit isn't worth someone's life! But for those on the top of the mountain, turning their backs on a dream that's so close they can see it is much harder. Plus, the incredible amounts of energy spent climbing the mountain stresses the body and impairs the mind—conditions that the defaults use to subvert your carefully laid plans and prevent you from reaching your true objectives.

Climbing Everest is a dramatic example of why it's important to implement execution fail-safes to ensure your decision gets executed as planned. Is it finally time to bail when you're running out of oxygen? Should you stay the course even though your other equipment is on its last legs? Execution fail-safes leverage your thinking when you're at your best to protect you against the defaults when you're at your worst.

The idea of an execution fail-safe is well illustrated by the Greek myth of Ulysses. Ulysses was the captain of his ship. He and his crew were navigating close to the island inhabited by the Sirens, dangerous creatures that lured sailors to their deaths with their song—a song so beautiful that it drove crews mad with longing till they ran their ships against the rocks trying to reach its source.

Ulysses wanted to hear the Sirens' song without risking the lives of his crew. Now, I'm not saying that Ulysses made a great decision here. If he'd really thought through his options using the principles and safeguards I've outlined, he would've steered clear of the island. But that's not the part I love about the story. What I love is that Ulysses implemented fail-safes to ensure his decision was executed as planned.

He stuffed the ears of his crew with beeswax so they couldn't hear the song as they approached the island. And to prevent them from changing course, he had them tie him to the mast so that no matter what he said or did in the madness of the song, he couldn't influence them or change the decision he'd already made. He also instructed them that the more he struggled and insisted on changing course, the tighter they should bind him.

Ulysses's clever implementation of execution fail-safes allowed him to hear the song while ensuring the safety of his crew. Of course, fail-safes are indispensable in a lot of other contexts too.

Three Kinds of Execution Fail-Safes

There are three kinds of execution fail-safes you should know: setting trip wires, empowering others to make decisions, and tying your hands.

> **FAIL-SAFE:** Set up trip wires to determine in advance what you'll do when you hit a specific quantifiable time, amount, or circumstance.

Trip wires are forms of precommitment—you commit yourself in advance to a course of action when certain conditions arise. For example, a team climbing Everest might set up a trip wire by committing themselves to abort their summit attempt if they don't reach a certain location by a certain time. If the team fails, they turn back! No argument. They don't try to decide in the midst of fatigue and oxygen deprivation; they've already decided and are already committed to turning around.

The path to success and failure is marked if you know where to look. The journey always contains the answers. Trip wires include both negative signs and the absence of positive signs. When the signs are positive, you know to stay the course. When things are murkier, however, that's when it helps to set trip wires.

Negative signs are red flags that something is going seriously off course. The sooner you catch yourself going the wrong way, the easier it is to turn back. The other day I ended up going east on the highway when I wanted to go west. Only when I noticed the wrong city was getting closer did I realize my mistake! But negative signs aren't the only ones to take note of. Sometimes the absence of positive signs is itself a sign.

When you don't see the positive signs you expected, it doesn't necessarily mean things have gone wrong. It does mean this is a moment worth paying attention to. Many projects fail, and many decisions get challenging right at this point—when people see neither negative signs nor the positive ones they expected. When that happens, it's time to re-evaluate. Ask yourself, "Is the most important thing still the most important thing? Was I wrong? What will it take to reach my goals now that I've moved further in time but not in progress?"

By having clear trip wires in place before you start, you

increase the odds of success. When the entire team understands clearly the markers of success and failure, they are empowered to act the minute things veer off course.

> **FAIL-SAFE:** Use commander's intent to empower others to act and make decisions without you.

Great leaders know that things don't always go according to plan. They also know they can't be everywhere at once. Teams need to know how to adapt when circumstances change. And circumstances change all the time.

Giving a team enough structure to carry out a mission but enough flexibility to respond to changing circumstances is called *commander's intent*—a military term first applied to the Germans who were trying to defeat Napoleon.

If you've ever been on the inside of a business where employees can't take action until everything is approved by their boss, you're seeing what happens without commander's intent. There's a single point of failure. If something happens to the boss, the business and mission fail.

Commander's intent empowers each person on a team to initiate and improvise as they're executing the plan. It stops you from being the bottleneck, and it enables the team to keep each other accountable to the goal without your presence.

Commander's intent has four components: formulate, communicate, interpret, and implement. The first two components—formulate and communicate—are the responsibility of the senior commander. You must communicate the strategy, the rationale, and the operational limits to the team. Tell them not just what to do, but why to do it, how you arrived at your decision, so they understand the context, as well as the boundaries for effective action—what is completely off the table. Subordinate commanders then have the tools for the last two components: interpreting the changing contexts and implementing the strategy in those contexts.

Before you begin executing a decision, just so there's no confusion as you move forward, ask yourself:

- Who needs to know my goals and the outcomes I'm working toward?
- Do they know what the most important objective is?
- Do they know the positive and negative signs to look for and what trip wires are attached to them?

One sign that you've failed to empower your team is that you can't be away from the office for a week without things falling apart. Some leaders think it makes them indispensable—that the team's inability to function without them is a sign of how important they are. Don't be fooled! This is the ego default at work. Effective leaders shouldn't have to be available 24/7 for their team to make decisions and achieve objectives. If you can't be away, it doesn't mean that you're indispensable or a supremely competent leader; it means that you're an incompetent communicator.

Another sign that you're in the grips of the ego default is that you insist on controlling how everything happens. Good leaders determine what needs to get done and set the parameters for getting there. They don't care whether something gets done differently from how they themselves would've done it. As long as it advances to the objective within the limits they've set, they're satisfied.

Poor leaders insist that everything must be done their way,

which ultimately demoralizes their team and undermines both loyalty and creativity—exactly the opposite of commander's intent.

FAIL-SAFE: Tie your hands to keep your execution on track.

Ulysses used trip wires and commander's intent to safeguard his decision. He also had the crew tie his hands—a final execution fail-safe to ensure he followed through with his decision, and the reason this kind of safeguard is known as a *Ulysses pact*.

Tying your hands amounts to different things in different contexts. If you're dieting, tying your hands might mean ridding your home of all junk food so there's nothing to tempt you. If you're investing, it might mean creating automated deposits each month. If you're climbing Everest, tying your hands might mean securing an agreement from everyone that the team will turn around if they don't reach the halfway point by a certain time.

Whatever decision you're facing, ask yourself, "Is there a way to make sure I will stick to the path I've decided is best?" By thinking through your options, and precommitting to courses of action, you free up space to tackle other problems.

Even if we're waiting as long as possible to decide, we now know exactly what to focus on and do when the time comes to make our decision. We've set our trip wires, we've empowered people to act on them, and we've tied our hands so that we can't undo all our good work in a moment of stress.

CHAPTER 4.6

Learn from Your Decisions

IF YOU'RE A KNOWLEDGE WORKER, YOU PRODUCE DECI-sions.[1] That's your job. The quality of your decisions eventu-ally determines how far you go and how fast you get there. If you learn to make great decisions consistently, you'll quickly move past the people whose decisions are merely good.

No one is smart enough to make great decisions without learning first, though. Great decision-makers have mastered the ability to learn both from their mistakes and from their successes. It's that ability that sets them apart. It enables them to repeat their successes and avoid repeating their failures. Un-less you develop that ability yourself, you won't improve your decision-making process over time.

A few years ago, a firm engaged me to help them improve the quality of their decisions. As a first step, we needed to find out where they were at. We started by trying to answer a sin-gle question: When their decision-makers expected a particu-lar result, how often did that result happen for the reasons they thought it would?

What we discovered shocked them: Their decision-makers

were right only about 20 percent of the time. Most of the time when something that they anticipated actually happened, it didn't happen for the reasons they thought it would. Their success, in other words, wasn't due to insight or effort or skill. It was more luck than skill. This news was a blow to their egos. They thought that the successes they enjoyed resulted largely from their abilities, but the numbers told a different story. They were like people getting lucky at roulette and attributing their success to having a "system."

The story illustrates a psychological phenomenon we've discussed before: *self-serving bias*, the tendency to evaluate things in ways that enhance our self-image. When we succeed at something, we tend to attribute our success to our ability or effort. By contrast, when we fail at something, we tend to attribute our failure to external factors. Basically, heads I'm right. Tails, I'm not wrong. If you want to get better, you have to rewrite the faulty narratives.

Self-serving bias gets in the way of learning from your decisions and improving your process. Our ego default wants us to think that we're smarter than we are and tells us that we work harder and know more than we actually do. The overconfidence that the ego demon inspires prevents us from examining our decisions with a critical eye. It keeps us from distinguishing skill from luck—what's in our control from what isn't. If you get trapped by the demon, you'll never learn from your decisions and never get better at making them in the future.

The first principle to keep in mind when evaluating your decisions is this:

> **THE PROCESS PRINCIPLE:** When you evaluate a decision, focus on the process you used to make the decision and not the outcome.

Conventional wisdom suggests that good outcomes result from good people making good decisions and bad outcomes result from bad people making bad decisions. But it's easy to find counterexamples. We've all made bad decisions, yet we're not all bad people. And even good decisions can have unexpected and unfortunate outcomes thanks to the necessary uncertainty of life.

Coach Pete Carroll of the Seattle Seahawks understands the difference between good decisions and good outcomes as well as anyone. In February 2015, Carroll made a historic call in the final minutes of Super Bowl XLIX that was immediately criticized as a huge mistake. The Seahawks trailed 28–24, but they were on New England's one-yard line and appeared certain to score and take the lead. Lined up in Seattle's backfield was Marshawn Lynch, a 215-pound battering ram who was arguably the most dominant running back in the NFL at the time, and who'd already run for more than one hundred yards against the Patriots that day. Here's a quick recap from a CBS Sports story that explains what happened next—and how Carroll's decisions continue to be viewed today:

> What transpired next will live in the annals of this league for as long as football games are played . . . a bizarre call by Carroll to throw on second down on a route in the crowded middle of the field will be second-guessed just as long—[and resulted] in Belichick and Tom Brady, the game's MVP, making history with their fourth Super Bowl title together.[2]

To the fans in the stands and nearly everyone watching the game, the right decision seemed obvious: just hand the ball to

"Beast Mode," as Lynch was known to many. But instead Carroll asked quarterback Russell Wilson to throw a pass, and the result was a disaster.

It's been years since this play. There's been a tremendous amount of analysis of it. Why didn't the coach make the easy choice that seemed so clear to everyone else? Based on good information, he was betting against his opponent's weaknesses. After the game, an interviewer told Carroll, "Everyone is thinking this was the greatest mistake of all time." Carroll's response: it was the "worst result of a call ever." His decision-making process was sound. It just didn't work out. Sometimes that's life.

The right call doesn't always get the intended outcome. Sooner or later everyone who makes decisions in the real world learns this lesson. Poker players know it. They can play their hand perfectly and still lose. Nothing is guaranteed. All you can do is play the hand you're dealt as best you can.

Carroll made his decision on the biggest stage in the world, and it had a terrible outcome. But his confidence in the decision was unwavering. Why? Because he knew the reasons why he had made the call. He knew his logic was sound. All he could do was learn from the outcome.

Many people assume that good decisions get good outcomes and bad ones don't. But that's not true. The quality of a single decision isn't determined by the quality of the outcome. Here's a thought experiment that will help illuminate this concept.

Imagine you engage in a very thoughtful and intentional decision-making process concerning your career. You have offers from a few different companies, one being a startup and another a Fortune 500. Based on where you are in your life, you decide to go with the Fortune 500 company. The pay is less up front, but it appears to be more stable.

Imagine your friend ends up working for the startup. You

watch as he gets raises and more vacation time. Is your decision good or bad?

Now, imagine the startup quickly folds after only a year. Does this affect how you feel about your decision?

I hope you get where I'm going with this. You can't control whether the startup takes off or not. Nor can you control in the moment how you feel about the startup offering higher pay. You can only control the process you use to make the decision. It's that process that determines whether a decision is good or bad. The quality of the outcome is a separate issue.

Our tendency to equate the quality of our decision with the outcome is called *resulting*. Results are the most visible part of a decision. Because of that, we tend to use them as an indicator of the decision's quality. If the results are what we wanted, we conclude that we made a good decision. If the results aren't what we wanted, we tend to blame external factors. It's not that our process was lacking; it's that a crucial bit of information was. (As opposed to when an acquaintance gets bad results, at which point we assume it's because they made a bad decision.)

Obviously, we all want good outcomes, but as we've seen, good decisions can have bad outcomes, and bad decisions can have good ones. Evaluating decisions—ours or others'—based on the outcome (or how we feel about the outcome) fails to distinguish luck from skill and control. Because of that, engaging in resulting doesn't help us get better. The result of resulting is instead stagnation.

If you've ever ruminated over a bad outcome—asking yourself again and again, "How did I not see that coming?"—then you've experienced how challenging and ultimately useless it is to judge your decisions on the basis of how you feel about them in retrospect. You think, "If only I had talked to that person (whom I didn't know at the time)!" or, "If I had only known that piece of information (which didn't exist at the time), I would have made the right choice." Even the best decision-makers get bad results from time to time, though.

Making a good decision is about the process, not the outcome. One bad outcome doesn't make you a poor decision-maker any more than one good outcome makes you a genius. Unless you evaluate your reasoning at the time you made the decision, you'll never know whether you were correct or just lucky. Your reasoning at that time remains mostly invisible unless you take steps to make it visible.

Rarely are you making decisions that have a 100 percent chance of success. And the kind of decision that has a 90 percent chance of success still has a bad outcome 10 percent of the time. What matters are results over time and ensuring that 10 percent of the time won't kill you.

The following matrix provides a way of organizing your reflection on decisions and their outcomes.

	Good outcome	Bad outcome
Good process	You make a good decision and things go as planned. You deserve the success you enjoy—you earned it. Don't let it go to your head. Stay on track and continue improving your process.	You make a good decision, but things don't go as planned. Bad luck! Don't get discouraged. Trust the process. Learn from the experience and continue improving.
Bad process	You make a bad decision but get lucky—like winning at roulette. Your success is undeserved. You did nothing to earn it. You just got lucky. Eventually you're going to lose. Change while you can. Grow up and take command of your decision-making.	You make a bad decision and are unlucky—like losing at roulette. You deserve failure. You earned it. Now learn from it. Let this be a wake-up call. Change while you can. Grow up and take command of your decision-making.

A bad process can never produce a good decision. Sure, it might result in a good outcome, but that's different from making a good decision. Outcomes are influenced in part by luck—both good and bad. Getting the right result for the wrong reasons isn't a function of smarts or skills, but just blind luck.

Don't get me wrong: it's nice to get lucky (provided you know it's luck). But luck isn't a repeatable process that secures good results over the long term. Luck isn't something you can learn, and it isn't something you can get better at. Luck won't give you an edge.

When you start equating luck with will, you're bound to make mistakes. You blind yourself to the risks you're taking, and are bound to be badly surprised sooner or later. And when you start confusing luck with skill, you're bound to squander opportunities to learn from your decisions, to improve your process, and to secure better results over the long term.

A second principle for evaluating your decisions in retrospect is this:

THE TRANSPARENCY PRINCIPLE: Make your decision-making process as visible and open to scrutiny as possible.

Evaluating other people's decisions is different from evaluating our own. We rarely see other people's intentions, thinking, or process, so it's hard judging their decisions by reference to anything other than their outcomes.

Evaluating our own decisions is different. We can have first-person insight into the process itself. We can examine our thinking, distinguish what was within our control from what wasn't, and what we knew at the time from what we didn't. We can then take what we've learned and invest it back into our process for next time. Of course, this is easier said than done!

Many of us have a hard time learning from our decisions. One reason is that our thinking and decision-making process is often invisible to us. We inadvertently conceal from ourselves the steps we took to reach our final decision. Once that decision gets made, we don't stop to reflect, but just move forward. And when we look back at our decision later, our ego manipulates our memories. We confuse what we know now with what we knew at the time we made the decision. And we see the outcomes and read them back into our intentions: "Oh, I meant to do that."

If you don't check your thinking at the time you made the decision—what you knew, what you thought was important, and how you reasoned about it—you'll never know whether you made a good decision or just got lucky. If you want to learn from decisions, you need to make the invisible thought process as visible and open to scrutiny as possible. The following safeguard can help:

> **SAFEGUARD:** *Keep a record of your thoughts at the time you make the decision.* Don't rely on your memory after the fact. Trying to recall what you knew and thought at the time you made the decision is a fool's game.

Your ego works to distort your memories and convinces you of narratives that make you feel smarter or more knowledgeable than you really are. No one, we think, could make better decisions than the ones we've made ourselves. The only way to see clearly what you were thinking at the time you made the decision is to keep a record of your thoughts at the time you were making the decision.

Writing down your thoughts offers several benefits. One benefit is that a written record provides information about your thought process at the time you made the decision. It makes the invisible visible. Later, when you reflect on your decision, having that record is helpful for counteracting the distorting effects of the ego default. You can truthfully answer questions like, "What did I know at the time I made the decision?" and, "Did the things I anticipated happening come about for the reasons I thought they would?"

A second benefit of recording your thoughts is that in the process of writing something, you often realize you don't really understand it as well as you thought you did. It's far better (and cheaper) to realize this before making your decision instead of after. If you do so in advance, you have an opportunity to get more information and a better grasp of the problem.

A third benefit to writing down your thoughts is that it allows other people to see your thinking, which is mostly invisible. And if they can see it, they can check it for errors and offer a different perspective that you might otherwise be blind to. If you can't simply explain your thinking to other people (or yourself), it's a sign that you don't fully understand things and need to dig deeper and gather more information.

A final benefit to writing down your thoughts is that it gives other people an opportunity to learn from your perspective. Many organizations would benefit from having a database that recorded how every person in the organization went about making decisions. Imagine the value of a searchable catalog of decisions in your organization. A system like this would allow people in different parts of the organization to check each other's thinking. It would allow management to distinguish good decision-makers from mediocre ones, and it would provide people with models of decision-making—both of how to do it and of how not to. If you build a system like this, I want an equity cut!

All of these principles will help you get what you want but not help you want what matters.

PART 5

WANTING
WHAT MATTERS

*Think of yourself as dead. You have
lived your life. Now take what's left
and live it properly.*

—MARCUS AURELIUS,
  Meditations, Book 7

GOOD DECISION-MAKING COMES down to two
things:

1. Knowing how to get what you want
2. Knowing what's worth wanting

The first point is about making effective decisions. The
second is about making good ones. You might think
they're the same, but they are not.

Decisions that bring immediate results, like closing a sale or filling a vacancy, may be effective, but they don't necessarily lead to the things that truly matter in life, like trust, love, and health. Good decisions, on the other hand, align with your long-term goals and values, and ultimately bring you the satisfaction and fulfillment that you truly desire in business, relationships, and life.*

Effective decisions get you the first outcome, while good ones get you the ultimate outcome.

All good decisions are effective, but not all effective decisions are good. Making the best judgments comes down to making decisions that get you what you really want—beyond just what you think you want at the moment.

In life, we experience regret over both things we've done and things we've failed to do. The worst regret is when we fail to live a life true to ourselves, when we fail to play by our own scoreboard.

Each default plays a role in setting us up for regret. The social default prompts us to inherit goals from other people, even if their life circumstances are very different from ours. The inertia default encourages us to continue pursuing the goals we've pursued in the past, even after we've come to realize that achieving them doesn't make us happy. The emotion default sends us this way and that, chasing whatever captures our fancy in the moment, even at the expense of pursuing long-term goals that matter more. And the ego default convinces us to pursue things like wealth, status, and power, even

---

*Assist from ChatGPT, whom I fed the original text of this paragraph to and asked to make it clearer!

at the expense of happiness and well-being—our own and that of the people around us.

If you give any of the defaults command of your life, your ultimate destination is regret. Don't live life by another person's scoreboard. Don't let someone else choose your objectives in life. Take responsibility for where you are and where you are headed.

Real wisdom doesn't come from chasing success but from building character. As Jim Collins wrote, "There is no effectiveness without discipline, and there is no discipline without character."[1]

•

Dickens's Hidden Lesson

EBENEZER SCROOGE IS ONE OF CHARLES DICKENS'S MOST memorable characters—an embodiment of greed and pursuing wealth at the expense of everything else. Scrooge is visited by three spirits who show him images of the past, the present, and a future that might be. In that future, Scrooge is dead, and the spirit allows him to eavesdrop on people's conversations about him: they're pleased Scrooge is gone, spiteful at his memory, unrepentant about stealing his things, and relieved that he's no longer a presence—a curse—in their lives. Scrooge sees the long-term consequences of the decisions he's made, regrets them, begs for a second chance, and gets an opportunity to change course.*

Scrooge played by society's scoreboard—the one that amplifies our biological instinct toward hierarchy and leads us to pursue money, status, and power at all costs. But his vision of the long-term future made him realize that none of these

---

* This is one of my favorite examples. Once Peter Kaufman pointed it out to me, I saw it everywhere.

things really mattered, that a life lived according to someone else's scoreboard is not a life worth living. He realized before it was too late that the key to a successful life is good company and meaningful relationships.

The quality of what you pursue determines the quality of your life. We think things like money, status, and power will make us happy, but they won't. The moment we get them, we're not satisfied. We just want more. The psychologists Philip Brickman and Donald T. Campbell coined a term for this phenomenon: *the hedonic treadmill*.[1] Who hasn't taken a run on it?

Remember when you were sixteen, and thought that if you just had a car, you'd be happy for the rest of your life? Then you got a car. For a week or two you were euphoric. You showed the car off to all your friends and drove it everywhere. You thought life was amazing. Then reality set in. Cars come with problems. In addition to paying for insurance, gas, and maintenance, there's also the problem of comparison. Back when you didn't have a car, you used to compare yourself with other people who didn't have cars. But now that you had a car, you began comparing yourself with other car owners. You noticed who had a better car, and were no longer happy with what had once made you ecstatic. You reverted to your old base-level discontent—the lowest gear on the hedonic treadmill. Comparison is the thief of joy.*

Social comparison happens all the time. Sometimes it's about possessions like houses or cars, but more often it's about status.

---

* This quote has been attributed to President Theodore Roosevelt, Mark Twain, and C. S. Lewis, but apparently none of them actually said it. See "Comparison Is the Thief of Joy," Quote Investigator, February 6, 2021, https://quoteinvestigator.com/2021/02/06/thief-of-joy/.

When I first started working in a large organization, the inner voice in my head told me that if I just got a promotion, I'd be happy. So I worked hard and got the promotion. For a few weeks I felt on top of the world. Then, much like with the car example, reality set in. I had new problems and new responsibilities. Worse, I started comparing myself with a new group of people. It wasn't long before I reverted to my previous level of discontent. Promotions continued to come, but none of them made me happier. They only left me wanting more.

We tell ourselves that the next level is enough, but it never is. The next zero in your bank account won't satisfy you any more than you are satisfied now. The next promotion won't change who you are. The fancy car won't make you happier. The bigger house doesn't solve your problems. More social media followers won't make you a better person.

Running on the hedonic treadmill only turns us into what I call "happy-when" people—those who think they'll be happy *when* something happens. For example, we'll be happy when we get the credit we deserve, or happy when we make a bit more money, or happy when we find that special someone. Happiness, however, isn't conditional.

Happy-when people are never actually happy. The moment they get what they think they want—the "when" part of the conditional—having that thing becomes the new norm, and they automatically want more. It's as if they've walked through a one-way door that closes behind them. Once the door closes, they lose perspective. They can't see where they've been, only where they are.

The way things are now is the way we expect them to be, and we start taking the good things around us for granted. Once that happens, nothing will make us happy. And while we're busy running on the treadmill chasing after all the things that won't make us happy, we're not pursuing the things that really matter.

Scrooge is a fictional example of achieving "success" at the cost of things that really matter. But there are many real examples. I once worked with someone who came to his position running a large company in a way that should be familiar to most of us: with sharp elbows in a hypercompetitive culture. The people he ran into on the way to becoming CEO were only means to help him achieve his ends: he wanted to be wealthy, he wanted to be respected, he wanted people to know his name. He wanted status and recognition.

After meetings, where things were tense and his temper got the better of him, he would often tell me, "Shane, you've got to decide if you're a lion or a sheep. I'm a lion," he'd say, and quote Tywin Lannister from *Game of Thrones*: "A lion doesn't concern himself with the opinions of a sheep." He wanted everyone to know he was at the top of the food chain.

An avid golfer, he often enjoyed several games a week. He never had trouble filling a round; in fact, he often complained that he had too many friends and couldn't play with them all. Shortly after retiring, he looked forward to finally having the time to enjoy his favorite pastime with his many friends. As it turned out, though, most of his "friends" and colleagues were busy, unavailable, or stopped returning his calls. He could hardly fill a single round a month.

His relationships had appeared real and meaningful, but in reality, no one wanted anything to do with him. His transactional way of handling other people made them feel used, manipulated, and frustrated. He yelled, cursed, and threw temper tantrums. They worked with him because they had to, not because they wanted to. Golfing was fun for him, but it was work for them.

A while after stepping away, he concluded that he'd been trying to win the wrong game. He'd aimed at achieving wealth, power, and prominence—the goals so many people tell us to pursue. He'd prioritized these goals above all others and pursued them relentlessly. In the end, he got what he thought he wanted. But it left him feeling empty. He achieved what he'd wanted at the expense of having meaningful relationships—which, he came to realize, was something that really mattered. Unlike Scrooge, he got no second chance.

How many of us—at whatever stages of our careers—are on the same trajectory? We value wealth and status more than happiness—the external more than the internal—and we give little thought to how we pursue them. In the process, we end up chasing praise and recognition from people who don't matter at the expense of people who do.

I've known many successful people whose lives I wouldn't want to have. They had intelligence, they had drive, they had opportunity, and the wherewithal to use them all. But they were missing something else. They knew how to get what they wanted, but the things they wanted weren't worth wanting. In fact, the things they wanted ended up disfiguring their lives. They were missing what Scrooge gains at the happy turning point of his story—that ingredient that makes the difference between the unhappy masses and the happy few.

The ancient Greeks had a word for this ingredient: *phronesis*—the wisdom of knowing how to order your life to achieve the best results.

When you look back to the decisions you made as a teenager, they probably seem pretty silly now. The time you stole (I mean *borrowed*) the car from your parents, the time you got too drunk at a party and maybe did some stuff you shouldn't have (thankfully there were no camera phones back then), the time you got into a fight with a friend over a potential mate. These decisions didn't seem stupid at the time so why do they appear so now? Because you have perspective now that was inaccessible to you back then. What seemed like the most important thing in the world at the time—the very thing that consumed you—seems silly now in hindsight.

Wisdom requires all the things we've talked about: the ability to keep the defaults in check, to create space for reason and reflection, to use the principles and safeguards that make for effective decisions. But being wise requires more. It's more than knowing how to get what you want. It's also knowing which things are worth wanting—which things really matter. It's as much about saying no as saying yes. We can't copy the life decisions of other people and expect better results. If we want to live the best life we can, we need a different approach.

Knowing what to want is the most important thing. Deep down, you already know what to do, you just need to follow your own advice. Sometimes, it's the advice we give other people that we most need to follow ourselves.

The Happiness Experts

I ONCE INTERVIEWED THE GERONTOLOGIST KARL PILLE-
mer, author of *30 Lessons for Living: Tried and True Advice from
the Wisest Americans.*[1] He'd seen numerous studies showing that
people in their seventies, eighties, and beyond were happier
than younger people. He was intrigued: "I kept meeting older
people—many of whom had lost loved ones, been through tremendous difficulties, and had serious health problems—but
who nevertheless were happy, fulfilled, and deeply enjoying
life. I found myself asking: 'What's that all about?'"

One day it hit him: Maybe older people just knew things
about living a happy life that younger people didn't. Maybe
they could see things we couldn't see. If any population demo-
graphic could lay claim to expertise in living a happy life, it
would be seniors. Yet to Pillemer's surprise, no one seemed to
have done a study on what practical advice older people had
for the younger generation. That set Pillemer off on a seven-
year quest to discover "the practical wisdom of older people."

Their number one lesson: life is short! "The older the respondent," Pillemer said, "the more likely [they were] to say

that life passes by in what seems like an instant." When elders tell younger people that life is short, they're not being macabre or pessimistic. They're instead trying to offer a perspective that they hope will inspire better decisions—ones that prioritize the things that really matter. "I wish I'd learned this in my 30s instead of in my 60s," one man told Pillemer, "I would have had so much more time to enjoy life." If only we could turn our future hindsight into our current foresight.

Time is the ultimate currency of life. The implications of managing the short time we have on earth are like those of managing any scarce resource: you have to use it wisely—in a way that prioritizes what's most important.

What were the most important things according to the people Pillemer interviewed? They included the following:

- Say things now to people you care about—whether it's expressing gratitude, asking forgiveness, or getting information.
- Spend the maximum amount of time with your children.
- Savor daily pleasures instead of waiting for "big-ticket items" to make you happy.
- Work in a job you love.
- Choose your mate carefully; don't just rush in.

The list of things they said weren't important was equally revealing:

- None said that to be happy you should work as hard as you can to get money.
- None said it was important to be as wealthy as the people around you.

- None said you should choose your career based on its earning potential.
- None said they regretted not getting even with someone who slighted them.

And the biggest regret people had? Worrying about things that never happened: "Worrying wastes your life," one respondent said.

These are important insights from the people that Pillemer describes as "the most credible experts we have on how to live happy and fulfilled lives during hard times." But there's another insight that's even more important.

Pillemer asked one of his interviewees for help understanding the source of her happiness. She thought about it and answered, "In my 89 years, I've learned that happiness is a choice—not a condition."

According to Pillemer, "The elders make the key distinction between events that happen to us, on the one hand, and our internal attitude toward happiness, on the other. Happy in spite of. Happiness is not a passive condition dependent on external events, nor is it the result of our personalities—just being born a happy person. Instead, happiness requires a conscious shift in outlook, in which one chooses—daily—optimism over pessimism, hope over despair."

The more we age, the more we come to see things the way Marcus Aurelius did: "When you are distressed by an external thing, it's not the thing itself that troubles you, but only your judgment of it. And you can wipe this out at a moment's notice."[2]

This insight has dramatic implications. It places happiness on a continuum with other decisions we've talked about.

Imagine that: all the decisions that make up your career and personal life ultimately add up to an overall decision to be happy. You can decide what to pursue in life. You can decide what's a priority for you. You can decide to channel your time, energy, and other resources toward things that really matter in the end.

If there were a way of viewing things from the perspective of our elders, we might have the insight to live better lives—to see in the way the experts do what really matters and what doesn't. In fact, there's an ancient technique for doing precisely this: start thinking about the shortness of life, and it will help you see what really matters.

"Let us prepare our minds as if we had come to the very end of life," Seneca said. If you want a better life, start thinking about death.

Memento Mori

LET'S DO A THOUGHT EXPERIMENT.

Clear your mind. Imagine you're eighty years old and nearing the end of your life. Maybe you have a couple years left, maybe just a couple hours. You're sitting on a park bench on a beautiful fall day overlooking a river. You hear the birds migrating above, the water flowing in the river, and the leaves falling off trees and gliding gently to the ground. Families are walking by, with parents holding the hands of their toddlers.

Take as long as you want. There is no rush.

Now think deeply. What's going on in the life you're imagining? Who are the people in it? In what ways have you influenced them? What have you done for them? How have you made them feel? What are the things you've accomplished? What possessions do you have? What matters most as you approach your final days? What seems unimportant? What memories do you cherish? What are the things you regret? What do your friends say about you? What about your family?

Shifting our perspective to the end of life can help us gain insight into what really matters. It can help us become wiser.

When we look back at the present through the lens of our life ending, the fears and desires that occupy our attention in the present moment get pushed aside to make room for things that have greater meaning for our lives as a whole. Steve Jobs put the idea this way:

> Remembering that I'll be dead soon is the most important tool I've ever encountered to help me make the big choices in life. Because almost everything—all external expectations, all pride, all fear of embarrassment or failure—these things just fall away in the face of death, leaving only what is truly important. Remembering that you are going to die is the best way I know to avoid the trap of thinking that you have something to lose.[1]

This shift in our perspective allows us to turn our future hindsight into our current foresight. It gives us a map we can use to navigate into the future. For many of us, looking at life this way reveals that our current direction isn't fully aligned with where we want to end up. Seeing that is a good thing! Knowing you're heading in the wrong direction is the first step toward getting back on course. When you get clear on what really matters, you can start asking yourself, "Am I making the right use of my limited time?"[2]

Jobs had a daily ritual. Every morning he would look in the mirror and ask himself, "If today were the last day of my life, would I want to do what I am about to do today?"[3] Whenever the answer was no too many days in a row, he said, he knew he needed to change something. At one point in my own life, I began performing the same ritual. It was part of the reason I eventually decided to leave the intelligence agency. We all have bad days, but when the answer to Job's question is no day after day, week after week, it's time to make a change.

When you did this exercise, you probably thought of your relationships. Maybe it was the time you and your spouse cried on the couch together, had a romantic weekend, or walked along a beach holding hands. Maybe it was your wedding. Or maybe it was a time you experienced pure joy with your kids. Maybe it was the time you were there for a friend or the time they were there for you.

Or perhaps your mind went toward your regrets—the opportunities you could have taken but didn't: the dreams you didn't chase, the business you didn't start, the love you didn't leap at, the trip you didn't go on, the way you held yourself back because you didn't want to get hurt, the time you were scared to do something different because you might look like a fool.

Jeff Bezos uses a similar thought experiment:

> I wanted to project myself forward to age 80 and say, "Okay, now I'm looking back on my life. I want to have minimized the number of regrets I have." . . . I knew that when I was 80 I was not going to regret having tried [Amazon]. I was not going to regret trying to participate in this thing called the Internet that I thought was going to be a really big deal. I knew that if I failed I wouldn't regret that, but I knew the one thing I might regret is not ever having tried. I knew that that would haunt me every day, and so, when I thought about it that way it was an incredibly easy decision.[4]

We regret the things we didn't do more than the things we did. The pain of trying and failing may be intense but at least it tends to be over rather quickly. The pain of failing to try, on the other hand, is less intense but never really goes away.[5]

Possessions become less important for what they are than for what they enable. I'm guessing that, in the thought exercise, you didn't think of your house as an investment. If it came to mind, it was probably in the context of the relationships and the memories—the family dinners, the laughs, the tears, the parties, the time you stayed in bed all day with your partner, the board game battles, the marks in the doorway that recorded how tall your kids were at each age.

I'm guessing you didn't think of the time you watched *Breaking Bad*, *The Mandalorian*, or *The Bachelor*. You probably didn't think of all the time you spent commuting and the extra podcasts or audiobooks you got to listen to. Perhaps you thought instead about how at least some of that time could have been used connecting with family and friends, or writing that book you always wanted to write.

You might remember the times you fell short of the person you wanted to be—we all have done so at one point or another. Perhaps it was the time you sent an inappropriate email, or the time you lost control of your emotions and yelled at someone you love. Maybe it was the time you said something you didn't mean just to cause a reaction in the other person because you didn't know how, in that moment, to tell them you loved them or how scared you were. Or perhaps it was the time someone said they needed you, and you were too busy with your own priorities to help.

You might think of the impact—or lack of it—that you had on your community, your city, your country, or the world. You might think of your health. Did you do everything you could to prepare your body to live to eighty, ninety, one hundred? Did you take care of yourself so you could take care of others?

What we think of as defining moments, like promotions or a new house, matter less to life satisfaction than the accumulation of tiny moments that didn't seem to matter at the time. In the end, everyday moments matter more than big prizes. Tiny delights over big bright lights.

Life Lessons from Death

It is not that we have a short time to live,
but that we waste a lot of it.

—SENECA,
On the Shortness of Life, Chapter 1

EVALUATING YOUR LIFE THROUGH THE LENS OF YOUR
death is raw, powerful, and perhaps a bit scary. What matters
most becomes clear. We become aware of the gap between
who we are and who we want to be. We see where we are and
where we want to go. Without that clarity, we lack wisdom
and waste the present on things that don't matter.

When I do this thought experiment, I gain a more objective perspective on my life. It makes me want to become a
better version of myself.

Initially, what comes to mind are the things I want to do
for others. Was I there when the people I love needed me? Did
I make time for the people closest to me? Am I the partner that
I want to be—loving, supportive, and true to my hopelessly

romantic and cheesy side? Was I a good father? Did I travel and see the world? Could people count on me? Was I an active participant in the community? Did I help people accomplish their dreams? Did I leave the world a better place?

When you know the destination, how to get there becomes clearer. As Aristotle says, "Knowledge of the best good carries great weight for knowing the best way to live: if we know it, then like archers who have a target to aim at, we are more likely to hit the right mark."[1]

At some point my kids figured out that it was easier to solve a maze backward than forward, especially if the maze is harder or more complicated than usual. Something about starting with the end in mind, they realized, makes it easier to decide which path to take. Life in general works similarly.

If this were your final year of life, would you be living the same way you are today? I posed this question to a friend of mine over lunch one day, and he quickly retorted, "I'd spend my savings, run up my credit cards, and start a drug habit." (He was joking about the drugs. I hope.)

When you think of your ninety-year-old self, it becomes clear that running up your credit card or doing drugs isn't going to make you happier. For many people, considering death makes us less likely to want to blow money.[2] (The downside of drugs is, I trust, self-explanatory.) And I'm sure you wouldn't spend your final year checking email, putting other people down, or trying to show your uncle just how right you were that one Thanksgiving when you argued about politics.

When you imagine your older self and what you want your life to look like in hindsight, you stop thinking about the small things that encourage you to be reactive instead of proactive. You start to see what actually matters to you. The small things look small, and the things that really matter start to look big.

From this perspective, it's easier to navigate toward the future you really want. You can see the gap between where you are and where you want to be, and change course if necessary.

For instance, after doing this thought experiment, I've started eating better, sleeping more, and exercising regularly. Why? Because in order to live to ninety and do all the things I aspire to, I need to be healthy. Likewise, after doing this thought experiment, it's clear that I want to be a more present father. Hence, I've cut back on my phone use around the kids and created routines that nudge connecting with them: every day when they come home, we sit on the couch and talk about the school day. No doubt these are small changes, but they have a big impact on me and the people that matter.

As I stick with the thought experiment, my mind wanders to what people will say about me after I'm gone, when there is no opportunity for me to respond. What will people *really* say?

Whatever it is, my opportunity to change it is right now—while I still have time.[3] Not all of what people say will be kind, so that means I have some relationships to repair. I can do that now, though. I can be the bigger person. Why? Because it matters to me.

Wisdom is turning your future hindsight into your current foresight. What seems to matter in the moment rarely matters in life, yet what matters in life always matters in the moment.[4]

What seems like winning in the moment is often just a shallow victory. It seems important at the time, but unimportant when you view it from the perspective of life as a whole. When we're not going in the direction in which we want to end up, we end up regretting where we end up. And avoiding regret is a key component to life satisfaction.

Good Judgment and the Good Life

Good judgment is, above all else, about being effective at achieving what matters—not what matters in the moment, but what matters in life. It's not about figuring out how to succeed today but understanding why and how we need to structure our lives with the end in mind. Good judgment is, above all else, having wisdom.

Wise people know what's really valuable. They know better than anyone that there's only one life—no rough draft, no do-over, no restart from an earlier save point. They don't squander their time chasing frivolous ambitions on a hedonic treadmill. They know what real wealth consists of, and they devote themselves to securing it—no matter what the crowd might think or say.

Sometimes the cost of being wise is that other people treat you like a fool. And no wonder: fools can't see what wise people do. Wise people see life in all its breadth: work, health, family, friends, faith, and community. They don't fixate on one part to the exclusion of others. They instead know how to harmonize life's various parts, and pursue each in proportion to the whole. They know that achieving harmony in that way is what makes life meaningful, admirable, and beautiful.

If you want to develop good judgment, start by asking two questions: "What do I want in life? And is what I want actually worth wanting?" Until you've answered the second question, all the decision-making advice in the world isn't going to do you much good. There's little profit in knowing how to get the things you want if those things won't make you happy. It doesn't matter how successful you become at acquiring power, fame, or money if at the end of it all you want a do-over.

The Value of Clear Thinking

GOOD JUDGMENT IS EXPENSIVE, BUT POOR JUDGMENT will cost you a fortune.

The overarching message of this book is that there are invisible instincts that conspire against good judgment. Your defaults encourage you to react without reasoning—to live unconsciously rather than deliberately.

When you revert to defaults, you engage in a game you can't win. When you live a life run on autopilot, you get bad results. You make things worse. You say things that can't be unsaid and do things that can't be undone. You might accomplish your immediate goal, but you fail to realize that you've made it harder to achieve your ultimate goals. All of this happens without consciously being aware you are exercising judgment in the first place.

Most books about thinking focus only on being more rational. They miss the fundamental problem: Most errors in judgment happen when we don't know we're supposed to be exercising judgment. They happen because our subconscious is driving our behaviors and cutting us out of the process of determining what we should do. You don't consciously choose to argue with your partner, but you find yourself saying hurtful things that can't be unsaid. You don't consciously seek money and status at the expense of your family, but you find yourself spending less and less time with the people who matter most in your life. You don't consciously seek to defend your ideas, but you find yourself holding grudges against anyone who criticizes you.

The key to getting what you want out of life is to identify how the world works and to align yourself with it. Often people think the world should work differently than it does, and when they don't get the outcomes they want, they try to wiggle out of responsibility by blaming other people or their circumstances.[1] Avoiding responsibility is a recipe for misery, and the opposite of what it takes to cultivate good judgment.

Improving your judgment, it turns out, is less about accumulating tools to enhance your rationality and more about implementing safeguards that make the desired path the path of least resistance. It's about designing systems when you're at your best that work for you when you're at your worst. Those systems don't eliminate the defaults, but they do help you recognize when they are running the show.

Managing your defaults requires more than willpower. Defaults operate at our subconscious level, so overriding them requires harnessing equally powerful forces that pull your subconscious in the right direction: habits, rules, and environment. Overriding your defaults requires implementing safeguards that render the invisible visible and that prevent you from acting too soon. And it requires cultivating habits of mind—accountability, knowledge, discipline, and confidence—that put you on the right track and keep you there.

The small improvements you make in judgment won't be

felt until they are too large to ignore. Gradually, as the improvements accumulate, you will notice that less of your time is spent fixing problems that shouldn't exist in the first place. You'll notice the various parts of your life blending harmoniously together, and you'll notice that you experience less stress and anxiety and more joy.

Good judgment can't be taught, but it can be learned.

Acknowledgments

THIS BOOK IS A SERIES OF THINGS THAT I HAVE LEARNED from others. Not only are the insights from others, but the work itself wouldn't be here without others.

I want to thank my incredible children, William and Mackenzie. Not only have they shown me the world through their endlessly curious eyes, but they've given me fertile ground to test these ideas in the real world.

I'm grateful to my parents for their support, encouragement, and never-ending belief in me. Mom and Dad, I love you. There were some challenging times, but we'll save that for another book. I got through it because of you. I also want to thank my high school English teacher Mr. Duncan, and high school bestie Scott Corkery, whose friendship (and family) forever changed my trajectory.

As for the content of the book, there are so many people to thank that I'm sure I will forget a few. Once you put a book out into the world, you can't change it, so you can find an updated list of thanks and appreciation at fs.blog.

I am fortunate to have learned from many people, but

perhaps no one has taught me more than Peter D. Kaufman. Many of the lessons and insights in this book come from our many conversations over the years. I am grateful for our friendship.

Charlie Munger, Warren Buffett, Andrew Wilkinson, Chris Sparling, James Clear, Ryan Holiday, Nir Eyal, Steve Kamb, Michael Kaumeyer, Morgan Housel, Michael Mauboussin, Alex Duncan, Kat Cole, Naval Ravikant, Jim Collins, Tobi Lütke, Annie Duke, Diana Chapman, and Randall Stutman have influenced my thoughts in meaningful ways. In fact, many of their thoughts have so firmly embedded themselves in me that they are indistinguishable from my own. To the extent you enjoy this book, you should look all of them up and follow them.

Writing a book is a marathon and not a sprint, and many people helped along the way. Thank you to Ariel Ratner, who got me started, and to William Jaworski, Ellen Fishbein, and Samuel Nightengale of Writing.coach. They spent so much time editing and transforming my sentences that some sections of the book are as much theirs as mine. Richelle DeVoe and the team at Pen Name helped organize and make real some of the threads in my head. We can all thank Joe Berkowitz for reducing the word count and getting rid of things that didn't need to be there.

I also want to thank early readers who provided insight and so much more: Trudy Boyle, Maureen Cunningham, Dr. Setareh Ziai, Rob Fraser, Zach Smith, Whitney Trujillo, Emily Segal, and Simon Eskildsen. And a big thanks to the team at FS for keeping everything going while I was working on this: Vicky Cosenzo, Rhiannon Beaubien, Dalton Mabery, Deb McGee, Laurie Lachance, and Alex Gheorghe.

Thanks to the team at Portfolio and Penguin Random

House who turned this into an actual thing. To the Michael Jordan of editing, Niki Papadopoulos, whose insight and patience as I missed every deadline was appreciated. And to my agent Rafe Sagalyn, who was instrumental in guiding me through the publishing process.

And . . . thank you. You've trusted me with something far more valuable than the price of this book; you've trusted me with your time. I hope your investment in the time to read this pays dividends for years to come.

Cheers.

Notes

Chapter 1.1

1. See, for instance, Aristotle's *Nicomachean Ethics*, second edition, translated by Terence Irwin (Indianapolis, IN: Hackett Publishing Company, 1999), pp. 18–19; Seneca's *Ad Lucilium Epistulae Morales* [*Moral Letters to Lucilius*], edited by Richard M. Gummere (New York: G. P. Putnam's Sons, 1917), Perseus Digital Library, text from Epistle 11 translated by William Jaworski: http://www .perseus.tufts.edu/hopper/text?doc=Sen.+Ep.+11&fromdoc =Perseus%3Atext%3A2007.01.0080; Daniel Kahneman's *Thinking, Fast and Slow* (New York: Farrar, Straus and Giroux, 2011); and Jonathan Haidt's *The Happiness Hypothesis: Finding Modern Truth in Ancient Wisdom* (New York: Basic Books, 2006).

2. This idea that we're naturally prone to defend our territory is an idea I came across through Robert Ardrey's book *The Territorial Imperative: A Personal Inquiry into the Animal Origins of Property and Nations*, as well as conversations with various people. While animals instinctively mark and defend their territory, I believe this biological instinct manifests itself in humans in a deeper and more nuanced way. We instinctively respond when people encroach on not only our physical territory but also our self-image. Since we wrap our identity into our jobs, when someone criticizes you at work, it's akin to an animal walking into your territory. Certain bad actors use this very fact to get you off your game—they'll criticize you or your role at the office in order to nudge you into reacting without reasoning.

3. "Hard-wired default" is a term that I first came across in David Foster Wallace's speech, "This Is Water," published in book form as *This Is Water: Some Thoughts, Delivered on a Significant Occasion, about Living a Compassionate Life* (New York: Little, Brown and Company, 2009).

Chapter 1.2

1. Associated Press, "American Anti Claims Silver," ESPN, August 22, 2004, https://www.espn.com/olympics/summer04/shooting /news/story?id=1864883.

Chapter 1.3

1. This idea of rushing to judgment with unearned knowledge is one I got from my friend Morgan Housel in "History's Seductive Beliefs," *Collab* (blog), Collaborative Fund, September 21, 2021, https://www.collabfund.com/blog/historys-seductive-beliefs/.
2. Hat tip to Kathryn Schulz, whose book, *Being Wrong: Adventures in the Margin of Error* (New York: Ecco, 2010), influenced my thinking.

Chapter 1.4

1. Robert P. George (@McCormickProf), Twitter, July 1, 2020, 11:23 p.m., https://twitter.com/mccormickprof/status /1278529694355292161.
2. This example comes from Paul Graham, "The Four Quadrants of Conformism," July 2020, http://www.paulgraham.com /conformism.html.
3. Paraphrasing Daniel Kahneman, *Thinking, Fast and Slow* (New York: Farrar, Straus and Giroux, 2011), p. 292.
4. Warren Buffett to Berkshire Hathaway shareholders, February 25, 1985, Berkshire Hathaway, https://www.berkshirehathaway.com /letters/1984.html.

Chapter 1.5

1. Shane Parrish and Rhiannon Beaubien, *The Great Mental Models*, vol. 2, *Physics, Chemistry and Biology* (Ottawa: Latticework Publishing, 2019).
2. Leonard Mlodinow, *Elastic: Flexible Thinking in a Time of Change* (New York: Pantheon, 2018), p. 156.

3. This misquotation was probably derived from Leon C. Megginson, professor of management and marketing at Louisiana State University at Baton Rouge. Even though Darwin himself never said it, the misattribution is now written in stone—literally! It adorns the floor of the California Academy of Sciences (although apparently the academy has now removed the attribution to Darwin). See "The Evolution of a Misquotation," Darwin Correspondence Project, University of Cambridge, https://www.darwinproject.ac.uk/people/about-darwin/six-things-darwin-never-said/evolution-misquotation.
4. Parrish and Beaubien, *The Great Mental Models*, vol. 2, pp. 76–77.

Chapter 2.1

1. Matt Rosoff, "Jeff Bezos Has Advice for the News Business: 'Ask People to Pay. They Will Pay,'" CNBC, June 21, 2017, https://www.cnbc.com/2017/06/21/jeff-bezos-lessons-from-washington-post-for-news-industry.html.
2. Reading and editing this today makes me think of the terrible and tragic case of Rehtaeh Parsons (who went to the same high school as me but at a different time) and her Facebook post "In the end, we will remember not the words of our enemies, but the silence of our friends." Tu Thanh Ha and Jane Taber, "Bullying Blamed in Death of Nova Scotia Teen," *Globe and Mail*, April 9, 2013, https://www.theglobeandmail.com/news/national/bullying-blamed-in-death-of-nova-scotia-teen/article10940600.

Chapter 2.4

1. Shane Parrish (@ShaneAParrish), "99.99 percent of the time waiting for the right moment to do something hard is how you rationalize not doing that hard thing you know you needs to be done. There is no perfect moment. All we have is now. Stop waiting," Twitter, July 29, 2019, 10:01 p.m., https://twitter.com/ShaneAParrish/status/1156021875853578246.
2. "The Wrong Side of Right," *Farnam Street* (blog), August 28, 2017, https://fs.blog/wrong-side-right/.

Chapter 2.6

1. Adam Wells, "Darrelle Revis Sent Home by Bill Belichick for Tardiness," Bleacher Report, October 22, 2014, https://

bleacherreport.com/articles/2241281-darrelle-revis-sent
-home-by-bill-belichick-for-tardiness.
2. "Haier: A Sledgehammer Start to Catfish Management,"
   IndustryWeek, October 13, 2013, https://www.industryweek.com
   /leadership/companies-executives/article/21961518/haier-a
   -sledgehammer-start-to-catfish-management.

Chapter 2.7

1. Seneca, *Moral Letters to Lucilius*, letter 11.
2. Shane Parrish, "Jim Collins: Relationships versus Transactions,"
   The Knowledge Project, podcast, episode 110, https://fs.blog
   /knowledge-project-podcast/jim-collins-2/.
3. Cato the Elder, *On Agriculture*, 1.
4. Shane Parrish, "The Work Required to Have an Opinion," *Farnam Street* (blog), April 29, 2013, https://fs.blog/the-work-required
   -to-have-an-opinion/.
5. From a private translation by William Jaworski of Michel de Montaigne, *The Essays of Michel de Montaigne*, book 3, chapter 12.
6. Denzel Washington, *A Hand to Guide Me* (Des Moines, IA: Meredith Books, 2006), p. 20.
7. Seneca, *Moral Letters to Lucilius*, letter 11.

Chapter 3.1

1. Richard Feynman, *The Pleasure of Finding Things Out: The Best Short Works of Richard P. Feynman*, ed. Jeffrey Robbins (New York: Basic Books, 1999), p. 212.
2. Michael Abrashoff, *It's Your Ship: Management Techniques from the Best Damn Ship in the Navy* (New York: Grand Central, 2002).
3. Abrashoff, *It's Your Ship*.

Chapter 3.2

1. Giora Keinan, Nehemia Friedland, and Yossef Ben-Porath,"Decision Making under Stress: Scanning of Alternatives under Physical Threat," *Acta Psychologica* 64, no. 3 (March 1987): 219–28.
2. Shane Parrish, "Daniel Kahneman: Putting Your Intuition On Ice," *The Knowledge Project*, podcast, episode 68, https://fs.blog
   /knowledge-project-podcast/daniel-kahneman/.

Chapter 4.1

1. Thomas Wedell-Wedellsborg, "Are You Solving the Right Problems?," *Harvard Business Review*, January–February 2017, https://hbr.org/2017/01/are-you-solving-the-right-problems.
2. I got the framing for this idea from Paul Graham (@paulg), "Something I told 12 yo and 8 yo on the way home from school: You can put your energy into being good at stuff or seeming cool, but not both. Any energy that goes into seeming cool comes out of being good," Twitter, March 12, 2021, 12:36 p.m., https://twitter.com/paulg/status/1370428561409073153.

Chapter 4.2

1. Jim Collins, *Good to Great: Why Some Companies Make the Leap . . . and Others Don't* (New York: HarperBusiness, 2001).
2. Seneca, *Moral Letters to Lucilius*, letter 91.
3. Josh Wolfe (@wolfejosh), "Failure comes from a failure to imagine failure. HORRID plan with unintended consequence increased screening amidst UNCERTAINTY #covid19—completely failed to anticipate—Increased crowds, decreased flow, increased CERTAINTY of SPREAD of any possible cases," Twitter, March 14, 2020, 9:51 p.m., https://twitter.com/wolfejosh/status/1239006370382393345?lang=en.
4. Special Inspector General for Afghanistan Reconstruction, *What We Need to Learn: Lessons from Twenty Years of Afghanistan Reconstruction*, August 2021, p. ix, https://www.sigar.mil/pdf/lessonslearned/SIGAR-21-46-LL.pdf.
5. Roger Martin, *The Opposable Mind: Winning through Integrative Thinking* (Boston: Harvard Business Press, 2009).
6. Charlie Munger, Berkshire Annual Meeting, 2003, quoted in Tren Griffin, *Charlie Munger: The Complete Investor* (New York: Columbia Business School Publishing, 2015).
7. Andrew Carnegie, *The Autobiography of Andrew Carnegie* (New York: PublicAffairs, 2011).

Chapter 4.3

1. "Remembering Roger Boisjoly: He Tried to Stop Shuttle Challenger Launch," NPR, *All Things Considered*, February 6, 2012, https://www.npr.org/sections/thetwo-way/2012/02/06/146490064/remembering-roger-boisjoly-he-tried-to-stop-shuttle-challenger-launch.

2. Tim Urban, "The Cook and the Chef: Musk's Secret Sauce," *Wait But Why* (blog), November 6, 2015, https://waitbutwhy.com/2015/11/the-cook-and-the-chef-musks-secret-sauce.html.

3. George C. Marshall: Interviews and Reminiscences for Forrest C. Pogue, tape 12m and tape 19m, November 21, 1956, George C. Marshall Foundation Research Library, Lexington, Virginia.

Chapter 4.4

1. Michael Lewis, *The Undoing Project: A Friendship That Changed Our Minds* (New York: W. W. Norton, 2016).

2. Shane Parrish "Winning at the Great Game with Adam Robinson (Part 2)," in *The Knowledge Project*, podcast, episode 48, https://fs.blog/knowledge-project-podcast/adam-robinson-pt2/.

Chapter 4.5

1. Karl Kaufman, "Here's Why Warren Buffett and Other Investors Don't Diversify," *Forbes*, July 24, 2018, https://www.forbes.com/sites/karlkaufman/2018/07/24/heres-why-warren-buffett-and-other-great-investors-dont-diversify/?sh=86081474795f.

2. Jim Collins and Morten T. Hansen, *Great by Choice: Uncertainty, Chaos, and Luck—Why Some Thrive Despite Them All* (New York: Harper Business, 2011).

3. Collins and Hansen, *Great by Choice*.

Chapter 4.6

1. "Your Product Is Decisions," *Farnam Street* (blog), November 27, 2013, https://fs.blog/your-product-is-decisions/.

2. Jason La Confora, "Super Bowl 49: Pete Carroll's Decision Astonishing, Explanation Perplexing," CBS Sports, February 1, 2015, https://www.cbssports.com/nfl/news/super-bowl-49-pete-carrolls-decision-astonishing-explanation-perplexing/.

Part 5

1. Jim Collins, foreword to *The 7 Habits of Highly Effective People: Powerful Lessons in Personal Change*, by Stephen R. Covey, 30th anniversary ed. (New York: Simon & Schuster, 2020).

Chapter 5.1

1. Philip Brickman and Donald T. Campbell, "Hedonic Relativism and Planning the Good Society," in *Adaptation-Level Theory: A*

Symposium, ed. M. H. Appley (New York: Academic Press, 1971), pp. 287–305.

Chapter 5.2

1. "Karl Pillemer, Interview No. 2," *Farnam Street* (blog), June 15, 2013, https://fs.blog/2013/06/karl-pillemer-interview-no-2/.
2. Marcus Aurelius, *Meditations* (New York: Modern Library, 2003), 8.47, Kindle.

Chapter 5.3

1. "'You've Got to Find What You Love,' Jobs Says," *Stanford News*, June 12, 2005, https://news.stanford.edu/2005/06/12/youve-got-find-love-jobs-says/.
2. This question is a play on "Am I making the right use of my scarce and precious life?" which I first heard from Arthur C. Brooks in "To Be Happier, Start Thinking More about Your Death," *New York Times*, January 9, 2016, https://www.nytimes.com/2016/01/10/opinion/sunday/to-be-happier-start-thinking-more-about-your-death.html.
3. "You've Got to Find What You Love," *Stanford News*.
4. Jeff Bezos, quoted in Jessica Stillman, "How Amazon's Jeff Bezos Made One of the Toughest Decisions of His Career," *Inc.*, June 13, 2016, https://www.inc.com/jessica-stillman/jeff-bezos-this-is-how-to-avoid-regret.html.
5. Shane Parrish (@ShaneAParrish), "The pain of trying and failing is intense and over rather quickly. The pain of failing to try, on the other hand, is less intense but never really goes away," Twitter, January 10, 2019, 10:53 p.m., https://twitter.com/ShaneAParrish/status/1083572670677938176.

Chapter 5.4

1. Aristotle, *Nicomachean Ethics*, book 1, chapter 2.
2. Nicholas J. Kelley and Brandon J. Schmeichel, "Thinking about Death Reduces Delay Discounting," *PLOS One*, December 2, 2015, https://doi.org/10.1371/journal.pone.0144228.
3. I got this idea originally from Drew Stegmaier, "Writing Your Own Eulogy," *Medium*, March 26, 2016, https://medium.com/the-mission/writing-your-own-eulogy-dd177ba45374.
4. I tested this on Twitter: Shane Parrish (@ShaneAParrish), "What matters in the moment rarely matters in life. Yet what matters in

life always matters in the moment," Twitter, December 7, 2019, 7:01 p.m., https://twitter.com/ShaneAParrish/status /1203464699305742336.

Conclusion

1. Borrowed from my work here: Shane Parrish, "Letting the World Do the Work for You," *Farnam Street* (blog), February 3, 2016, https://fs.blog/joseph-tussman/.

Index

Index

bullets before cannonballs approach,
200–202

Campbell, Donald T., 226
Carnegie, Andrew, 151
Carroll, Pete, 213–14
Cato the Elder, 84
Challenger space shuttle, 157
change, 30–32
changing your mind, 33
    about what you think you know,
        67, 68
character, 223
checklists, 109
choices, vs. decisions, 119–22
clapping, 23
clarity, in defining criteria, 156
Clear, James, 91, 94n
clear thinking, viii, x, xiii–xv, 245–47
Cole, Kat, x
Collins, Jim, 83, 135, 200, 223
commander's intent, 206, 208–10
comparison, social, 226–27
complaining, 52
complexity, 27n
computer algorithms, 35–37, 91
confidence, *see* self-confidence
confirmation bias, 191
conflict, avoiding, 33
consequentiality, 184–85
control, cost of losing, 6–7
COVID pandemic, 20n
criteria, 155–59, 161
    assigning quantitative values to,
        163–64
    most important, defining, 159–61

Darwin, Charles, 32
death, life lessons from, 234, 235–39,
    240–43
decisions, viii, x, xiv, 119–23
    big, focusing on, xiii
    choices vs., 119–22
    consequences of, 184–85
    empowering others to make, 206,
        208–10
    evaluation in, *see* evaluation stage
    execution of, *see* action

good vs. effective, 221–22
learning from, 211–20
    keeping a record of how you made
        the decision, 218–20
    Process Principle and, 212–17
    Transparency Principle and, 217–18
living with, before announcing,
    203–4
ordinary moments and, xiii–xv
problem-defining stage in, *see*
    problem-defining stage
process in, 120–21
results of, 215
reversibility of, 184–85
solution-exploring stage in, *see*
    solution-exploring stage
decisiveness, 156, 158–59
defaulting to clarity, 35–37
defaults, 6, 10–11, 35, 36, 39–40, 94,
    222–23, 245, 246
    ego, 10–11, 16–22, 30, 48, 50, 52,
        70, 95, 97, 114, 159, 166, 183,
        196, 209, 212, 218, 222–23
    and appearing successful vs. being
        successful, 17–20
    and feeling right vs. being right,
        21–22
    emotion, 10–11, 12–15, 59–60, 95,
        156, 222
    mistakes and, 116
    inertia, 10–11, 29–34, 40, 93, 95,
        114, 158, 183
    and doubling down when you're
        wrong, 32–34
    in groups, 33, 34
    self-knowledge about, 58
    social, 10–11, 23–28, 126, 127, 131,
        134, 156, 158, 183, 196, 222
    and deviating from established
        practices, 25–28
    resisting, 72–73
defining the problem, *see* problem-
    defining stage
Descartes, René, 30n
Dickens, Charles, Ebenezer Scrooge
    character of, 225–26, 228, 229
Discourses (Epictetus), 74
dog adoptions, 129–30, 133

262

Index

Index

NASA, 157
Nero, 23n
New England Patriots, 76, 213
Newton, Isaac, 30
Nicomachean Ethics (Aristotle), 87
norm, going against, 71–72

On the Shortness of Life (Seneca), 240
On the Tranquility of the Mind (Seneca), 84
opinion, vs. information, 172–73
opportunity costs, 150–54
   Opportunity Cost Principle in, 152
   3-Lens Principle in, 152–54
options
   diminishing, 192
   evaluating, *see* evaluation stage
   information about, *see* information
ordinary moments, xiii–xv, 6

Peart, Neil, 119
perspective, shifting, 110–12
pet adoptions, 129–30, 133
phronesis, 229
Pillemer, Karl, 231–33
Pixel Union, 162
positioning, xiv–xv
premortem, 137, 138
prevention, 102–3
Princeton Review, 190
problem(s)
   anticipating, 137–39
   exploring solutions to, *see* solution-exploring stage
   writing out, 132
problem-defining stage, 120, 125–34
   Definition Principle in, 128, 130
   Root Cause Principle and, 128–30
   safeguarding of, 130–34
      problem-solution firewall, 130–32
      test of time, 133–34
Process Principle, 212–17
Propaganda (Bernays), 29

quiet quitting, 20n

Ravikant, Naval, 181n
Reagan, Ronald, 157

reason and rationality, 5–6, 60, 245
Redelmeier, Don, 187–88
Reed, Joseph, 19–20
regrets, 233, 237, 242
relationships, 226, 228
responsibility, 43, 44, 48–50, 53, 158, 223, 246
   for mistakes, 115–17
   see also self-accountability
results, 215
reversibility, 184–85
Revis, Darrelle, 76
rewards, 43, 44
right, the wrong side of, 21–22, 50, 67–70
rituals, 40, 73n
Robinson, Adam, x, 190, 191
Rohn, Jim, 94n
role models, *see* exemplars
Root Cause Principle, 128–30
rules, automatic, 72, 103–7
Rumsfeld, Donald, 56

safeguards, 95, 101–12, 246
   automatic rules, 72, 103–7
   in evaluation stage, 161–64
   friction, 107–9
   guardrails, 109–10
   for HiFi information, 171–75
      asking people how they think, 173–75
      evaluating motivations and incentives of sources, 172–73
      running an experiment, 171–72
   keeping a record of how you made decisions, 218–20
   perspective, 110–12
   prevention, 102–3
   in problem-defining stage, 130–34
      problem-solution firewall, 130–32
      test of time, 133–34
   in solution-exploring stage, 145–50
      Both-And options, 148–50
      imagining one option as off the table, 146–47
sandbox metaphor, 88–89
Schopenhauer, Arthur, 35

Index

Scrooge, Ebenezer, 225–26, 228, 229
Seattle Seahawks, 213–14
Second-Level Thinking Principle,
    139–45
self-accountability, 41, 43–55, 71–73
    blame and, 44, 48, 52, 53, 113, 246
    complaining and, 52
    excuses and, 44–47
    and responses making things better
      or worse, 50–51
    responsibility and, 43, 44, 48–50, 53,
      115–17, 158, 223, 246
    victimhood and, 52–55
self-confidence, 17–18, 41, 62–70,
    71–73, 95
    ego vs., 63
    honesty and, 66–68
    and how you talk to yourself, 63–65
    and wrong side of right, 67–70
self-control, 41, 59–61, 71–73, 95
self-defense and territoriality, 8, 10, 39,
    46–47, 93
self-image, 46–47, 50
self-knowledge, 41, 56–58, 63, 71–73
    defaults and, 58
self-preservation, 9, 10, 39, 48n, 93
self-serving bias, 48, 113, 212
Seneca, 82, 84, 87, 137, 138, 234, 240
Shakespeare, William, 59
Sharp, Isadore, 149
Shippen, Peggy, 19
Shopify, 85, 162
Slovic, Paul, 190
social comparison, 226–27
social default, 10–11, 23–28, 126,
    127, 131, 134, 156, 158, 183,
    196, 222
    and deviating from established
      practices, 25–28
    resisting, 72–73
social hierarchies, 9, 10, 18, 21, 30n,
    39, 93
social pressure, 23–24, 95
solution-exploring stage, 120,
    135–54, 155
    Bad Outcome Principle and,
      138–39, 143
    opportunity costs and, 150–54

Opportunity Cost Principle in, 152
3-Lens Principle in, 152–54
safeguarding of, 145–50
    Both-And options, 148–50
    imagining one option as off the
      table, 146–47
    Second-Level Thinking Principle
      and, 139–45
    separating problem-defining phase
      from, 130–32
    3+ Principle and, 146
Stakes of Diplomacy, The (Lippmann),
    23
standards, 74–79, 88
    low, reasons for, 78
    low, smart people with, 76–78
Stockdale, James, 135–36
Stoics, 8
Stop, FLOP, Know Principle, 190–92
strength(s), 41
    in action, 71–73
    building, 39–41, 95
    knowledge about, 56, 58
stress, 102
Stutman, Randall, x
successes, learning from, 211
successful, appearing vs. being, 17–20
Super Bowl XLIX, 213–14
Syrus, Publilius, 49

Taleb, Nassim, 167n, 199
Targeting Principle, 164–65
Temple of Apollo at Delphi, 56
Thiokol, Morton, 157
30 Lessons for Living (Pillemer), 231
3-Lens Principle, 152–54
3+ Principle, 146
time, xv, 232
    test of, 133–34
trade-offs, 150–51
Transparency Principle, 217–18
trip wires, 206–8, 210
Tuft & Needle, 172
tying your hands, 206, 210

Ulysses, 205–6, 210
Undoing Project, The (Lewis), 187
Urban, Tim, 167

266

The Brain Food
Newsletter

Get a mental edge in five minutes
with weekly wisdom you can use.
For free.

`fs.blog/newsletter`